Quick and Easy Thai Recipes

Jean-Pierre Gabriel

Quick and Easy Thai Recipes

Introduction

Thailand's bright, fresh food is inimitable—and needn't be ordered only from your favorite local Thai restaurant. After a quick shopping trip to an Asian grocery, and a bagful of good, fresh produce, it's a snap to cook. *Quick and Easy Thai Recipes* features the tastiest dishes from all over Thailand, including soups, dips, curries, noodles, stir-fries, drinks, and even desserts—all ready in thirty minutes or less.

The country itself is often compared to an elephant head seen in profile, sandwiched among other nations: Its forehead tilts toward Myanmar and its ears are laced by Laos and Cambodia. And indeed, Thai cuisine owes much to foreign influences: The pad Thai and "drunken noodles" we know and love from take-out (take away) menus owe much to Chinese immigrants, and the chilis and tomatoes dotting curries and salads came to Southeast Asia via Spanish and Portuguese settlers.

One thing often forgotten in the discussion of Thailand's cuisine is its connection to the dominant Thai religion. In the before-dawn hours, a visitor might see lines of Buddhist monks, glowing in saffron-colored robes, slowly gathering the culinary offerings made by the faithful. Thai dining rituals are so connected to this faith that certain holidays—such as Songkran, an annual festival with Buddhist roots—are the only times local families might make particular dishes.

Happily, though, Thai dishes can be made at home, whenever you want, without much effort. Look for the savory noodles, salads, and curries you know and love, but also remember that desserts—fried bananas, tapioca, and a light coconut milk–melon concoction—are a hallmark of Thai cuisine, and some of the best in the world. You may never order takeout again.

Pastes and Sauces

Its pastes and sauces are perhaps Thai cuisine's most iconic foods. Think of the sweet, peanuty satay slathered over a chicken skewer hot off the grill, or the fried garlic you remember shellacked onto sticky-sweet Thai-style wings. Try these simple condiments dolloped on rice and noodles, and start to notice repeat cameos from the garlic, shallots, ginger, galangal, and cilantro (coriander) ubiquitous in markets across Thailand. Once you've started cooking with tamarind and lime (for sourness), chilis (for spice), palm sugar (for sweetness), shrimp paste and fish sauce (for salt), you're well on your way to Thai food expertise.

Fermented Soybeans

Makes 8 small packages
Cook time: 10 minutes, plus
  fermenting time

— 2 cups (10 oz/300 g) canned soybeans,
  drained
— 8 banana leaves

Divide the soybeans into 8 portions and put each portion in the center of a banana leaf. Cover the soybeans with the sides of the leaf, fold over the ends, and secure with string. Place a weight on top of the packages and let ferment at room temperature for 2–3 days.

The fermented soybeans are then ready to use.

To make dried soybean sheets, remove the soybeans from the banana leaves and shape into balls. Flatten into thin rounds and sun-dry for 2–3 days.

Cucumber Relish

Makes 1 cup (8 oz/230 g)
Cook time: 20 minutes

— ½ cup (120 ml) white vinegar
— ⅔ cup (140 g) granulated sugar
— ¼ teaspoon salt
— 1 small cucumber (2 oz/50 g), halved
   lengthwise and thinly sliced
— 2 shallots, thinly sliced
— 1 fresh red bird's eye chili, sliced

Put the vinegar, sugar, and salt in a small pan and set over medium-low heat. Stir until the sugar has dissolved. Bring to a boil and cook for about 4 minutes, or until the mixture turns slightly syrupy. Remove from the heat and let cool completely. Add the cucumber, shallots, and chili and serve.

If not serving right away, store airtight in the refrigerator for up to 3 days.

Chili Jam

Makes 1 cup (12 oz/338 g)
Cook time: 30 minutes

— 15 dried red bird's eye chilis, seeded
— 8 cloves garlic, unpeeled and halved
— 2–3 shallots, coarsely chopped
— 1 teaspoon salt
— ¼ cup (0.25 oz/10 g) dried shrimp, pounded
— 1 teaspoon shrimp paste
— ½ cup (120 ml) vegetable oil
— 1 tablespoon Tamarind Puree (page 32)
— 1 tablespoon fish sauce
— 2½ tablespoons jaggery, palm sugar, or light brown sugar

Dry-fry the dried chilis in a wok over medium heat for 3–4 minutes, until fragrant and toasted. Transfer to a plate and set aside. Add the garlic and shallots to the wok and dry-fry over medium heat for 5–6 minutes, until softened and the garlic skins are slightly burned. Remove from the wok and set aside.

Using a mortar and pestle, pound the toasted chilis with the salt until ground to fine flakes. Add the garlic and shallots and pound until smooth. Add the dried shrimp and shrimp paste and pound until smooth and thoroughly combined. (Alternatively, combine the ingredients in a food processor and pulse to form a smooth paste.)

Heat the oil in the wok over medium heat. Add the paste and cook for 2–3 minutes, until fragrant. Add the tamarind, fish sauce, and sugar and stir for about 4 minutes, or until fully flavored.

If not using right away, store airtight in the refrigerator for up to 2 weeks.

Roasted Shrimp Paste

Makes ¼ cup (2 oz/60 g)
Cook time: 10 minutes

— 1 banana leaf, for wrapping
— 4 tablespoons shrimp paste

Lay the banana leaf on a work surface, spoon the shrimp paste into the center of the leaf, and gently press to flatten the shrimp paste. Cover the paste with the sides of the leaf, fold over the ends, and secure with a toothpick.

Hold the banana-leaf package over a low gas flame for about 5 minutes, turning it from time to time until the leaf is charred and the shrimp paste is fragrant. (Alternatively, preheat the oven to 400°F/200°C/Gas Mark 6 and roast the banana leaf package for about 10 minutes, or until fragrant.)

If not using right away, store airtight in the refrigerator for up to 1 week.

Larb Chili Paste

Makes 1 cup (8 oz/210 g)
Cook time: 20 minutes

— 5–10 dried red bird's eye chilis,
  seeded
— 3 shallots, halved
— 3 cloves garlic
— 10 fresh long red peppers, chopped
— 2 tablespoons finely chopped
  lemongrass
— 1 tablespoon dill seeds
— 1 tablespoon fennel seeds
— 1 tablespoon Sichuan peppercorns
— ½ tablespoon cardamom pods
— 1 teaspoon ground nutmeg
— ¼ teaspoon whole cloves
— ¼ teaspoon cumin seeds
— 3 dried red chilis
— ½ teaspoon salt

Dry-fry the dried bird's eye chilis in a wok over medium heat for 2–3 minutes, until fragrant. Remove and set aside.

Add the shallots, garlic, and long peppers to the same wok and dry-fry for about 2 minutes, or until softened and golden brown. Remove and set aside. Dry-fry the lemongrass, dill seeds, fennel seeds, Sichuan peppercorns, cardamom pods, nutmeg, cloves, and cumin seeds in the wok for 3–4 minutes, until fragrant and toasted. Remove and let cool.

Pound the dried chilis and salt together in a mortar with a pestle until fine flakes. Add the fried chilis, shallots, garlic, and long peppers and pound until smooth. Gradually add the remaining toasted ingredients and continue pounding until smooth. (Alternatively, combine the ingredients in a food processor and pulse to form a smooth paste.)

If not using right away, store airtight in the refrigerator for up to 3 weeks.

Dry Curry Paste

Makes ½ cup (3 oz/90 g)
Cook time: 10 minutes, plus soaking time

— 5 dried bird's eye chilis, seeded
— ½ teaspoon salt
— 1 tablespoon sliced lemongrass
— 1 teaspoon sliced galangal
— 1½ teaspoons grated kaffir lime zest
— 4–5 small shallots
— 6 cloves garlic
— 1 teaspoon sliced cilantro (coriander) root*
— ½ teaspoon black peppercorns
— ½ teaspoon ground coriander
— 1 teaspoon ground cumin
— ½ teaspoon ground cardamom
— 1 teaspoon shrimp paste

*   If you can't find cilantro with the roots still attached, just use the stems and double the quantity called for.

Soak the dried chilis in a bowl of warm water for 15 minutes or until rehydrated, then drain and chop.

Pound the chilis and salt in a mortar with a pestle until fine flakes form. Add the lemongrass, galangal, kaffir zest, whole shallots, garlic, cilantro root, peppercorns, ground coriander, cumin, and cardamom and pound again until smooth.

Add the shrimp paste and pound until combined. (Alternatively, combine the ingredients in a food processor and pulse to form a smooth paste.)

If not using right away, store airtight in the refrigerator for up to 3 weeks.

Red Curry Paste

Makes ½ cup (4 oz/120 g)
Cook time: 10 minutes, plus soaking time

— 14 dried red bird's eye chilis, seeded
— 1 teaspoon ground coriander
— ½ teaspoon ground cumin
— 1 teaspoon white peppercorns
— 1 teaspoon salt
— 1 teaspoon chopped galangal
— ½ teaspoon chopped cilantro
   (coriander) root*
— 1 tablespoon finely chopped or grated
   kaffir lime zest
— ¼ cup (0.5 oz/15 g) finely sliced
   lemongrass
— 1½ shallots, chopped
— 4 cloves garlic
— 1½ teaspoons shrimp paste

*   *If you can't find cilantro with the*
   roots still attached, just use the stems
   and double the quantity called for.

Soak the dried chilis in a bowl of warm water for 15 minutes or until rehydrated, then drain and chop. Set aside.

Toast the coriander and cumin in a small pan over medium heat for 1 minute, or until fragrant. Transfer to a mortar, add the white peppercorns, and pound with a pestle until the peppercorns are finely ground. Remove from the mortar and set aside. (Alternatively, combine the ingredients in a spice grinder and pulse until finely ground.)

Add the chopped chilis and salt to the mortar and pound until smooth. Gradually add the galangal, cilantro root, kaffir lime zest, lemongrass, shallots, and garlic and continue to pound until smooth. Add the shrimp paste and toasted spice mix and pound until smooth and thoroughly combined. (Alternatively, combine the ingredients in a food processor and pulse to form a smooth paste.)

If not using right away, store airtight in the refrigerator for up to 3 weeks.

Southern Chili Paste

Makes ½ cup (6 oz/170 g)
Cook time: 10 minutes, plus soaking time

— 10–15 dried red bird's eye chilis,
  seeded
— 1 teaspoon salt
— 3 stalks lemongrass, thinly sliced
— 3 thin slices galangal
— 1 teaspoon black peppercorns
— 1½ teaspoons chopped fresh turmeric
  or ½ teaspoon ground turmeric
— 4 cloves garlic, chopped
— 2 small shallots, sliced
— 2 teaspoons shrimp paste

Soak the dried chilis in a bowl of warm water for 15 minutes or until rehydrated, then drain and chop.

Transfer the chopped chilis to a mortar with the salt and pound with a pestle until it forms fine flakes. Gradually add the lemongrass, galangal, peppercorns, turmeric, garlic, and shallots and pound until smooth. Add the shrimp paste and pound until smooth and thoroughly combined. (Alternatively, combine the ingredients in a food processor and pulse to form a smooth paste.)

If not using right away, store airtight in the refrigerator for up to 4 weeks.

Saam-gler

Makes 3 tablespoons (1 oz/32 g)
Cook time: 10 minutes

— 1 cup (0.5 oz/15 g) cilantro
  (coriander) roots*
— 4 cloves garlic
— 2 teaspoons black or white
  peppercorns

* *If you can't find cilantro with the*
  roots still attached, just use the stems
  and double the quantity called for.

Pound the cilantro root briefly in a mortar with a pestle. Add the garlic and continue to pound until a coarse paste. Add the peppercorns and pound to a fine paste. (Alternatively, combine the ingredients in a food processor and pulse to form a fine paste.)

If not using right away, store airtight in the refrigerator for up to 3 weeks.

Spicy Green Mango Dip

Makes 1 cup (250 ml)
Cook time: 10 minutes

— 5–10 fresh green bird's eye chilis, chopped
— 3 cloves garlic, chopped
— 1 tablespoon jaggery, palm sugar, or light brown sugar
— 2 teaspoons Roasted Shrimp Paste (page 13)
— ½ cup (3 oz/80 g) shredded unripe green mango or green apple, plus extra to garnish
— 2 tablespoons dried shrimp, coarsely pounded
— 2½ teaspoons fish sauce
— 1 tablespoon fresh lime juice
— vegetables, such as cauliflower and cucumber, for serving

Pound the chilis and garlic in a mortar with a pestle until smooth. Add the sugar and shrimp paste and continue to pound until combined. Add the mango or apple, dried shrimp, fish sauce, lime juice, and 2 tablespoons warm water and gently mix. (Alternatively, combine the ingredients in a food processor and pulse until roughly chopped and combined, but not a smooth puree.)

Garnish with shredded mango or apple and serve with raw vegetables.

Chili Dip

Makes 2 cups (475 ml)
Cook time: 15 minutes, plus soaking time

For the chili paste
— 2 oz/50 g dried red chilis, seeded
— 2 bulbs garlic, cloves separated
   and peeled
— 5 shallots, chopped
— 1½ cups (4 oz/100 g) finely
   chopped lemongrass
— 4-inch/10 cm piece red galangal,
   peeled and finely chopped
— 1 teaspoon whole green cardamom
   pods
— 4 oz/100 g dried shrimp
— ⅓ cup (2.25 oz/60 g) shrimp paste

For the dip
— 2 cups (475 ml) coconut milk
— ¼ cup (50 g) jaggery, palm sugar,
   or light brown sugar
— 2 teaspoons salt
— 5 kaffir lime leaves, chopped
— raw or steamed vegetables, such
   as cucumber and round eggplants
   (aubergines), for serving

To make the chili paste, soak the dried chilis in a bowl of hot water for 15 minutes, or until rehydrated, then drain.

Pound the chilis, garlic, shallots, lemongrass, red galangal, and cardamom pods together in a mortar with a pestle until smooth. Add the dried shrimp and shrimp paste and pound again until combined. (Alternatively, combine the ingredients in a food processor and pulse to form a smooth paste.)

For the dip, bring the coconut milk to a boil in a wok over medium heat and boil for 4–5 minutes, until a grainy texture forms. Add the chili paste, sugar, salt, and kaffir lime leaves and simmer for 3–4 minutes.

Transfer to a bowl and serve with raw or steamed vegetables.

Shrimp Paste Dipping Sauce

Makes 1¼ cups (300 ml)
Cook time: 15 minutes

— 1½ tablespoons Red Curry Paste
  (page 16)
— 2 stalks lemongrass, thinly sliced
— ¾-inch/2 cm piece fingerroot or
  ginger, peeled and julienned
— 1 shallot, sliced
— 1½ tablespoons Roasted Shrimp
  Paste (page 13)
— 0.25 oz/10 g salted mackerel
— 1 tablespoon vegetable oil
— scant 1 cup (200 ml) coconut milk
— 2 tablespoons jaggery, palm sugar,
  or light brown sugar
— 1 teaspoon fish sauce
— 1 tablespoon Tamarind Puree
  (page 32)
— 7 fresh green bird's eye chilis,
  crushed
— 4 kaffir lime leaves, torn
— raw or steamed vegetables, such as
  carrots, napa (Chinese) cabbage,
  cucumbers, and yard-long beans,
  for serving

For the garnish
— 1 fresh green chili
— 1 sprig cilantro (coriander)
— 1 fresh red bird's eye chili, slivered

Pound the curry paste with the lemongrass, fingerroot, shallot, shrimp paste, and salted mackerel in a mortar with a pestle until smooth. (Alternatively, combine the ingredients in a food processor and pulse to form a smooth paste.)

Heat the oil in a wok over medium heat. Add the pounded paste and stir-fry for about 3 minutes, or until fragrant. Add the coconut milk and stir constantly until thickened. Add the sugar, fish sauce, and tamarind and stir until thoroughly combined.

Add the crushed chilis and kaffir lime leaves, stir, and remove from the heat. Transfer to a bowl and garnish with the whole green chili, cilantro sprig, and red chili slivers. Serve with raw or steamed vegetables.

Seafood Dipping Sauce

Makes ¾ cup (175 ml)
Cook time: 5 minutes

— 6–7 cloves garlic
— 10 fresh red and green bird's eye chilis
— ½ cup (20 g) coarsely chopped cilantro
  (coriander)
— 3 tablespoons fish sauce
— 2 tablespoons jaggery, palm sugar,
  or light brown sugar
— 2 tablespoons fresh lime juice
— broiled (grilled) or steamed seafood,
  for serving

Pound the garlic in a mortar with a pestle. Add the chilis and pound into fine pieces. Add the cilantro and pound until smooth. (Alternatively, combine the ingredients in a food processor and pulse to form a smooth paste.) Add the fish sauce, sugar, lime juice, and 1 tablespoon water and stir with a spoon until the sugar has dissolved. It should be sweet, sour, salty, and hot. Serve in a bowl with broiled or steamed seafood.

If not serving right away, store airtight in the refrigerator for up to 2 weeks.

Very Spicy Thai Dipping Sauce

Makes 1¼ cups (300 ml)
Cook time: 10 minutes

— 20 cloves garlic
— 30 fresh red bird's eye chilis, chopped
— ½ cup (120 ml) fish sauce
— ½ cup (120 ml) fresh lime juice
— broiled (grilled) meat or fish, for
   serving

Pound the garlic and chilis to a smooth paste in a mortar with a pestle. (Alternatively, combine the ingredients in a food processor and pulse to form a smooth paste.) Transfer to a bowl, add the fish sauce and lime juice, and mix well until thoroughly combined. Serve with broiled meat or fish.

Sweet Chili Dipping Sauce

Makes ¾ cup (175 ml)
Cook time: 15 minutes

— ½ cup (120 ml) white vinegar
— ½ cup (100 g) granulated sugar
— ½ teaspoon salt
— 1 fresh red chili, coarsely pounded
— 2 tablespoons coarsely chopped
   peanuts, for garnish (optional)

Mix the vinegar, sugar, salt, 4 tablespoons water, and the red chili together in a pan. Bring to a boil and cook for 2 minutes. Reduce the heat to low and simmer for another 3–5 minutes, until it becomes a syrupy consistency. Remove from the heat and let cool. Serve, garnished with peanuts if desired.

If not using right away, let cool, then store airtight in the refrigerator for up to 1 week.

Thai-Style Satay Sauce

Makes 1 cup (250 ml)
Cook time: 15 minutes

— 1 tablespoon vegetable oil
— 1 tablespoon Dry Curry Paste (page 15)
— scant 1 cup (200 ml) coconut milk
— ⅔ cup (4 oz/100 g) roasted peanuts,
  finely crushed
— 3 tablespoons jaggery, palm sugar, or
  light brown sugar
— ¼ teaspoon salt
— ½ teaspoon Tamarind Puree (page 32)

Heat the oil in a wok over medium heat. Add the curry paste and sauté for 30 seconds, or until it sizzles and becomes fragrant. Gradually add the coconut milk, stir, and let boil for 2–3 minutes. Add the peanuts, sugar, salt, and tamarind, and stir for 3–4 minutes. Remove from the heat and transfer to a serving bowl.

Tamarind Puree

Makes 2½ cups (550 ml)
Cook time: 15 minutes

— 1 lb 2 oz/500 g sour tamarind pods,
   peeled and seeded

Mix 2 cups (475 ml) warm water with the tamarind pulp in a large bowl, then knead together by hand. Strain the mixture through cheesecloth (muslin) into a large bowl.

If not using right away, store airtight in the refrigerator for up to 1 week.

Fried Garlic

Makes 5 tablespoons
Cook time: 10 minutes

— 1½ cups (350 ml) vegetable oil
— 2 bulbs garlic, cloves separated,
  peeled, and sliced

Heat the oil in a wok over medium heat. Add the garlic and stir-fry for 4–5 minutes, until the garlic starts to brown. Remove with a slotted spoon and drain on paper towels. Use as an ingredient or a garnish.

Fried Shallots

Makes 5 tablespoons
Cook time: 15 minutes

— 1½ cups (350 ml) vegetable oil
— 5 shallots, peeled and thinly sliced
   lengthwise

Heat the oil in a wok over medium heat. Add the shallots and stir-fry for 10–11 minutes, until the shallots start to brown. Remove with a slotted spoon and drain on paper towels. Use as an ingredient or a garnish.

Snacks and Drinks

Try lemongrass—that flavor familiar to anyone who loves Thai food—in a whole new way, juiced up with sugar and ice for the most refreshing concoction you've had in a while. It's one of several excellent, supersimple Thai drinks in this section, including kumquat juice, passion fruit juice, and a dragon fruit frappé. You'll also spy some familiar favorites, such as spring rolls and Thai omelets (which are so much easier than you'd think!) Serving a freshly made juice along with dinner can take it from weekday-worthy to a memorable meal with friends.

Broiled Eggs in Banana Leaves

Serves 4–6
Cook time: 30 minutes

— 2 lb 4 oz/1 kg banana leaves, cut into rounds 6 inches/15 cm in diameter
— 5 eggs
— 2 fresh red bird's eye chilis, chopped
— 2 tablespoons soy sauce
— 2 tablespoons chopped cilantro (coriander)
— ½ teaspoon salt

Prepare the banana-leaf cups. For each cup, place 2 banana leaf rounds back to back with the shiny surface facing outward on both sides. From the outside of the round, fold up about 1¼ inches/ 3 cm of banana leaf and then fold in on itself to create a corner. Secure with a toothpick or use a stapler. Repeat until there are 4 corners. Set aside.

Heat the broiler (grill) to low. Put the eggs, chilis, soy sauce, cilantro, and salt into a large bowl and mix well until combined. Add 1–3 tablespoons water while mixing the eggs to make the texture softer. Carefully pour about ½ cup (120 ml) of the egg mixture into each banana leaf cup.

Put the banana leaf cups on the broiler rack and broil for 15 minutes, or until the eggs are cooked through.

Herb Omelet

Serves 2
Cook time: 10 minutes

— 3 eggs, beaten
— 4 oz/100 g ground (minced) pork
  or chicken
— 5 cloves garlic, chopped
— 2 scallions (spring onions), chopped
— handful of cilantro (coriander),
  chopped
— 2 shallots, chopped
— ¼ teaspoon salt
— 7 fresh red bird's eye chilis, chopped
— ¼ teaspoon ground white pepper
— 1 teaspoon soy sauce
— 1 teaspoon oyster sauce
— 3 tablespoons vegetable oil
— Steamed Jasmine Rice (page 204),
  for serving

Whisk the eggs with all the ingredients (except the oil and rice) in a large bowl until combined.

Heat the oil in a frying pan over medium-low heat. Add the egg mixture and cook for 3–4 minutes, until the underside starts to set and the meat is browned. When almost cooked, carefully flip the omelet over and cook for 1–2 minutes to quickly color the other side. Serve on its own or with rice.

Thai Spring Rolls

Makes 20 rolls
Cook time: 25 minutes

For the sauce
— 1 cup (250 ml) Tamarind Puree
   (page 32)
— 5 dried chilis, soaked
— 3 shallots
— 1 tablespoon soy sauce
— ½ cup (100 g) jaggery, palm sugar,
   or light brown sugar
— 7 cloves garlic
— 1 tablespoon Fermented Soybeans
   (page 10)

For the spring rolls
— 1 tablespoon vegetable oil
— 1 cup (4 oz/120 g) shredded jicama
— 2 tablespoons oyster sauce
— 20 spring roll wrapper sheets
— 2 cups (4 oz/120 g) shredded lettuce
— 2 cups (4 oz/120 g) boiled bean
   sprouts
— 1 cup (0.5 oz/15 g) crispy pork rind,
   coarsely chopped
— 2 tablespoons Fried Shallots (page 34)
— 4 oz/100 g roasted pork, thinly sliced
— 20 cooked shrimp (prawns), halved
   lengthwise

To make the sauce, pound all the ingredients together in a mortar with a pestle until smooth. (Alternatively, combine the ingredients in a food processor and pulse to form a smooth paste.) Heat the sauce in a wok over medium heat, bring to a boil, then reduce the heat and simmer until thickened. Remove from the heat and cool.

To make the spring rolls, heat the oil in a wok over medium heat. Add the jicama and oyster sauce and sauté for 30 seconds. Remove from the heat and set aside to cool.

Soften a spring roll wrapper in warm water and lay out on a work surface. Put a little of the lettuce, bean sprouts, pork rind, fried shallots, and jicama in the center of the wrapper. Add a little sauce and top with a slice of roasted pork and 2–3 shrimp slices. Fold the bottom of the wrapper up and over the filling. Fold the left and right sides in to create a package. Roll the package up toward the top and brush a little water on the top edges of the wrapper to stick the package together. Repeat until you have used up all the fillings. Cut the rolls in half and serve with the remaining sauce.

Pork and Shrimp on Pineapple

Serves 4–6
Cook time: 30 minutes

— 8 cloves garlic
— 5 cilantro (coriander) roots*
— ½ teaspoon ground white pepper
— 3 tablespoons vegetable oil
— ¾ cup (150 g) jaggery, palm sugar,
  or light brown sugar
— 1½ teaspoons salt
— 4 oz/100 g ground (minced) pork
— 4 oz/100 g raw shrimp (prawns),
  peeled, deveined, and ground (minced)
— 1 cup (5 oz/150 g) roasted peanuts,
  crushed
— 1 pineapple, peeled, cored, and cut
  into 1¼ × ½-inch/3 × 1 cm pieces
— handful of cilantro leaves
— 1 fresh red bird's eye chili, finely
  sliced

* *If you can't find cilantro with the*
  roots still attached, just use the stems
  and double the quantity called for.

Finely pound the garlic, cilantro root, and pepper in a mortar with a pestle. (Alternatively, combine the ingredients in a food processor and pulse to form a smooth paste.)

Heat the oil in a wok over medium-low heat. Add the garlic paste and sauté for 2–3 minutes, until golden and fragrant. Add the sugar and salt and cook for another 2–3 minutes, until the sugar softens. Add the pork and shrimp and cook for another 4 minutes. Stir in the peanuts and cook for 8–9 minutes, until everything starts to become sticky. Remove the wok from the heat and let cool.

When cool enough to handle, shape the mixture into ¾-inch/2 cm balls and place each ball onto an individual piece of pineapple. Top each ball with a cilantro leaf and a slice of chili, and serve.

Dragon Fruit Frappé

Serves 4
Cook time: 10 minutes

— 4 dragon fruits, peeled and chopped
— 8 ice cubes
— 2 tablespoons honey
— 2 teaspoons fresh lime juice

Put the dragon fruits into a blender, add the ice cubes, honey, and lime juice and blend until smooth. Serve.

Passion Fruit Juice

Serves 4
Cook time: 10 minutes

— 1 cup (200 g) superfine (caster) sugar
— 2 lb 4 oz/1 kg passion fruit, halved, or
    18 oz/500 g frozen passion fruit puree
— 1 teaspoon salt
— ice cubes, for serving

Bring 1½ cups (350 ml) water to a boil in a large pan over medium heat. Add the sugar and stir until the sugar has dissolved and the mixture has become syrupy, then remove from the heat.

Strain the passion fruit through a piece of cheesecloth (muslin) into a large heatproof pitcher (jug) and discard the solids. (Alternatively, whisk the passion fruit puree.) Add the salt and ½ cup (120 ml) sugar syrup and stir well. Serve cold over ice.

Store the remaining syrup airtight in the refrigerator for up to 3 weeks.

Kumquat Juice

Serves 8–10
Cook time: 15 minutes

— 2 lb 4 oz/1 kg kumquats or 18 oz/
   500 g frozen kumquat puree
— 5 cups (1 kg) superfine (caster) sugar
— 1 tablespoon salt
— ice cubes, for serving

Wash the kumquats and squeeze the juice into a large pan. Pour in 8½ cups (2 liters) water and stir until mixed. Add the sugar and salt, then bring to a boil over medium heat. Remove from the heat, strain through a piece of cheesecloth (muslin) into a large heatproof pitcher (jug), and let cool. (Alternatively, combine 8½ cups [2 liters] water with the sugar in a large pan and stir until mixed. Add the salt, then bring to a boil over medium heat. Remove from the heat when mixture is slightly syrupy, stir in the fruit puree. Strain into a large heatproof pitcher, and let cool.) Refrigerate the juice to chill. Serve cold over ice.

Snacks and Drinks

Lemongrass Juice

Serves 6–8
Cook time: 25 minutes

— 1 lb 2 oz/500 g chopped lemongrass
  stalks
— 1½ cups (300 g) superfine (caster)
  sugar
— ½ teaspoon salt
— ice cubes, for serving

Bring 8½ cups (2 liters) water to a boil in a large pan over medium heat. Add the lemongrass and simmer for 8–10 minutes. Remove from the heat and strain the lemongrass juice through a piece of cheesecloth (muslin) into a large clean pan. Add the sugar and salt, stir until dissolved, and bring to a boil over medium heat. Remove from the heat and let cool, then refrigerate to chill. Serve cold over ice.

Pandan Juice

Serves 4–6
Cook time: 15 minutes

— 6 oz/170 g pandan leaves (about 5),
  washed and cut crosswise into
  2–3-inch/5–8 cm lengths
— ¼ cup (50 g) granulated sugar
— pinch of salt
— ice cubes, for serving (optional)

Bring 6 cups (1.4 liters) water to a boil in a large
pan over medium-high heat. Add the pandan
leaves, reduce the heat to medium-low, and boil
for 5 minutes. Add the sugar and salt and boil for
another 2–3 minutes until the sugar and salt have
dissolved. Remove from the heat and adjust the
sweetness to taste. Pour the mixture through
a fine sieve into a heatproof pitcher (jug).

Serve hot or refrigerate to chill and serve cold
over ice.

Tamarind Juice

Serves 4
Cook time: 15 minutes, plus soaking time

— ⅓ cup (3 oz/80 g) pulp from sour
  tamarind pods or sour tamarind paste
— ¼ teaspoon salt
— 1¼ cups (250 g) granulated sugar
— ice cubes, for serving

Soak the tamarind pulp or paste in 1½ cups (350 ml) warm water: 15–20 minutes for pulp, 10 minutes for paste. Squeeze the tamarind and water together with your hands until you have quite a thick puree. Strain the tamarind mixture through a fine sieve into a cup. Set aside.

Bring 4 cups (950 ml) water to a boil in a pan over medium heat. Add the tamarind puree, salt, and sugar and stir until the sugar has dissolved, then boil for 4–5 minutes. Remove from the heat. Serve hot or refrigerate to chill and serve cold over ice.

Salads

Papaya salad is one of those addictive restaurant dishes
we crave mightily at times and think is beyond our reach
as home cooks. Not so, and it's among the easier salads in
this section, nestled alongside similarly simple dishes such
as a spicy shrimp and pork salad, a mango salad, and a spicy
squid and heart of palm concoction that will delight both the
heat seeker and the seafood lover in your home. This is the
food you want to warm you up in the dead of winter and help
you sweat through the middle of summer—deliciously.

Spicy Salted Egg Salad

Serves 2
Cook time: 15 minutes

— 5–6 fresh red bird's eye chilis
— 3–4 cloves garlic
— 1 yard-long bean, cut into 3-inch/
  1¼ cm lengths
— 3 small plum tomatoes, halved
— 6 oz/175 g julienned green papaya
  (about 1 cup)
— 2 tablespoons dried shrimp
— 1–2 tablespoons fresh lime juice
— 1 tablespoon jaggery, palm sugar,
  or light brown sugar
— 1 tablespoon fish sauce
— 2 salted duck eggs, cooked,
  quartered lengthwise, for garnish
— 2 tablespoons roasted peanuts,
  for garnish

Coarsely pound the chilis and garlic in a mortar with a pestle. Add the bean, tomatoes, papaya, and dried shrimp and mix together. Season with the lime juice to taste, sugar, and fish sauce and mix well. Transfer to a serving dish and garnish with the egg. Sprinkle with the peanuts and serve.

Spicy Squid and Heart of Palm Salad

Serves 6
Cook time: 20 minutes

For the dressing
— 2½ tablespoons fish sauce
— 2 tablespoons fresh lime juice
— 1½ tablespoons granulated sugar
— 10 fresh red bird's eye chilis, finely
  chopped

For the salad
— 11 oz/300 g squid, cleaned and cut
  into 1½-inch/4 cm pieces
— 4 oz/100 g raw shrimp (prawns),
  peeled and deveined, tails still intact
— 5 oz/150 g hearts of palm, julienned
— ½ cup (3 oz/80 g) julienned unripe
  green mango, green papaya, or jicama
— 1 cup (4 oz/100 g) shredded carrots
— 1 onion, sliced lengthwise
— 4 tablespoons chopped cilantro
  (coriander)
— 5 scallions (spring onions), sliced
  lengthwise

For the dressing, mix the fish sauce, lime juice, sugar, and chilis together in a large bowl until the sugar has dissolved. Set aside

For the salad, blanch the squid in a pan of boiling water for 2–3 minutes, until cooked. Drain and set aside.

Blanch the shrimp in another pan of boiling water for 1–2 minutes, until pink. Drain and set aside.

Add the squid, shrimp, hearts of palm, mango, carrots, onion, cilantro, and scallions to the bowl of dressing and mix well. Serve.

Deep-Fried Squid Salad

Serves 2
Cook time: 20 minutes

— ⅔ cup (75 g) all-purpose (plain) flour
— 2 cups (475 ml) vegetable oil, for
  deep-frying
— 11 oz/300 g squid, cut into rings
  ½ inch/1 cm thick
— 2 tablespoons Chili Jam (page 12)
— 2 tablespoons fresh lime juice
— 2 tablespoons fish sauce
— ½ teaspoon granulated sugar
— 1 shallot, sliced
— 3 kaffir lime leaves, finely sliced
— 5 fresh red bird's eye chilis, chopped
— 2 stalks lemongrass, finely sliced
— mint leaves, for garnish

Whisk together the flour and ½ cup (120 ml) cold water in a bowl until thoroughly combined. Set aside.

Heat the oil in a wok or deep-fryer to 350°F/180°C or until a cube of bread browns in 30 seconds. Dip the squid into the batter, then carefully put the squid in the hot oil and deep-fry for 4–6 minutes, until golden and crispy. Remove with a slotted spoon and drain on paper towels.

Mix the chili jam, lime juice, fish sauce, sugar, shallot, kaffir lime leaves, chilis, and lemongrass together in a bowl. Add the squid and mix well. Transfer to a serving plate, garnish with the mint leaves, and serve.

Spicy Hummingbird Flower Salad

Serves 4
Cook time: 20 minutes

For the dressing, pound the chilis and garlic in a mortar with a pestle, then add the fish sauce, lime juice, and sugar and mix well. Transfer to a large serving bowl and set aside.

For the dressing
— 10 fresh red and green bird's eye chilis, chopped
— 1 clove garlic, chopped
— 2 tablespoons fish sauce
— 2 tablespoons fresh lime juice
— 1 tablespoon granulated sugar

For the salad
— 11 oz/300 g raw shrimp (prawns), peeled and deveined, with tails still intact
— 7 oz/200 g ground (minced) pork
— 1 lb 2 oz/500 g vegetable hummingbird flowers, stamens removed, or squash blossoms
— 10 shallots, minced

For the salad, blanch the shrimp in a pan of boiling water for 1–2 minutes or until pink. Drain and set aside.

Blanch the ground pork in another pan of boiling water for 2–3 minutes, or until cooked. Drain well and set aside.

Blanch the vegetable hummingbird flowers in a third pan of boiling water for 1 minute. Drain and set aside.

Add the shrimp, pork, and hummingbird flowers to the bowl of dressing and mix well. Stir in the minced shallots and serve.

Cilantro Salad

Serves 2
Cook time: 20 minutes, plus soaking time

For the chili paste
— 7 dried red chilis
— 7 cloves garlic
— 4 slices fresh ginger
— 5 shallots, chopped
— 2 slices galangal or ginger
— 2 stalks lemongrass
— 3 cilantro (coriander) roots*
— 1 teaspoon shrimp paste
— 2 tablespoons vegetable oil

For the salad
— 1 cup (2 oz/50 g) finely sliced cilantro
— 2 cups (4 oz/100 g) pork crackling,
    coarsely chopped
— 3 tablespoons Fried Garlic (page 33)
— 3 tablespoons Fried Shallots (page 34)
— salt

* *If you can't find cilantro with the*
  roots still attached, just use the stems
  and double the quantity called for.

To make the chili paste, soak the dried chilis in a bowl of warm water for 15 minutes or until rehydrated, then drain and chop.

Pound the chilis, garlic, ginger, shallots, galangal, lemongrass, cilantro roots, and shrimp paste thoroughly in a mortar with a pestle. (Alternatively, combine the ingredients in a food processor and pulse to form a smooth paste.)

Heat the oil in a wok over medium heat. Add the chili paste and stir-fry for 2 minutes, or until fragrant. Remove from the heat.

To make the salad, put the cilantro and the pork crackling in a bowl and mix well. Add the chili paste and a of pinch salt and mix well. Sprinkle with the fried garlic and shallots and serve.

Pickled Vegetable Salad

Serves 4
Cook time: 10 minutes

— 5 fresh red bird's eye chilis
— 1 cup (4 oz/120 g) sliced pickled
  mustard greens
— 2 yellow or green round eggplants
  (aubergines), sliced
— 1½-inch/4 cm piece fresh ginger,
  peeled and sliced

Leave 3 chilis whole and finely chop the rest. Set aside.

Mix the pickled mustard greens, eggplants, and ginger together in a large bowl. Sprinkle with the whole and finely chopped chilis. Serve.

Spicy Mushroom Salad

Serves 4
Cook time: 15 minutes

For the dressing
— 3 tablespoons fish sauce
— 3 tablespoons fresh lime juice
— 5–6 fresh bird's eye chilis, finely
  chopped
— 1½ tablespoons jaggery, palm sugar,
  or light brown sugar

For the salad
— 4 oz/100 g ground (minced) pork
— 8–10 raw jumbo shrimp (king prawns),
  peeled and deveined
— 11 oz/300 g mixed mushrooms, such
  as straw, king oyster, and shimeji
— 1 tablespoon finely chopped scallions
  (spring onions)
— 4–5 shallots, finely sliced
— handful of cilantro (coriander),
  coarsely chopped, for garnish

For the dressing, stir the fish sauce, lime juice, chilis, and sugar together in a large bowl until the sugar has dissolved. Set aside.

For the salad, blanch the pork in a pan of boiling water for 2–3 minutes, until cooked. Drain and set aside.

Blanch the shrimp in another pan of boiling water for 1–2 minutes. Drain and set aside.

Blanch the mushrooms in a third pan of boiling water for about 30 seconds. Drain and set aside.

Add the pork, shrimp, mushrooms, scallions, and shallots to the bowl of dressing and mix well. Transfer to a serving plate, sprinkle with the cilantro, and serve.

Pomelo Salad

Serves 4
Cook time: 10 minutes

— 1⅓ cups (4 oz/100 g) unsweetened
  shredded (desiccated) coconut
— ⅓ cup (2 oz/50 g) peanuts
— 1 lb 2 oz/500 g pomelo or red
  grapefruits
— 2½ cups (4 oz/100 g) dried shrimp,
  rinsed
— 1 shallot, finely chopped
— 2 tablespoons fish sauce
— 3 tablespoons granulated sugar

Dry-fry the coconut and peanuts in a wok over medium heat for 2–3 minutes, until golden brown. Remove and set aside.

Peel the pomelo and cut it into segments. Remove and discard the spongy pith and membranes, then break the flesh into small pieces and transfer to a large bowl. (If using grapefruits, slice off a piece at the top and bottom and use a sharp knife to follow the curve of the fruit and remove the peel, pith, and membranes to expose the fruit. Cut the segments of grapefruit flesh out of their membranes and chop.)

Add the coconut, peanuts, dried shrimp, and shallot to the bowl and mix well. Add the fish sauce and sugar and mix well. Serve.

Green Papaya Salad

Serves 2
Cook time: 15 minutes

— 3 fresh bird's eye chilis
— 5 cloves garlic
— 1 yard-long bean, cut into 1½-inch/
  4 cm lengths
— 2 plum tomatoes, diced
— 1 tablespoon jaggery, palm sugar,
  or light brown sugar
— 1 tablespoon roasted peanuts
— 1 tablespoon dried shrimp
— 1 tablespoon fresh lime juice
— 2 limes, cut into wedges
— 1 tablespoon fish sauce
— ⅔ cup (4 oz/120 g) julienned green
  papaya, green mango, or jicama

Pound the chilis and garlic together in a mortar with a pestle. Add the bean and lightly crush. Add the tomatoes, sugar, roasted peanuts, dried shrimp, lime juice, lime wedges, and fish sauce to the mortar and gently mix together until the sugar has dissolved. Add the papaya and mix together. Serve.

Mango Salad with Smoked Dried Fish

Serves 2
Cook time: 10 minutes

— 1½ teaspoons rice flour
— 1 cup (5 oz/165 g) julienned unripe
    green mango, green papaya, or jicama
— 2 tablespoons smoked dried fish, finely
    pounded
— 1½ teaspoons dried chili flakes
— 1 tablespoon fish sauce
— 2 scallions (spring onions), cut into
    1½-inch/4 cm lengths
— ½ cup (1 oz/25 g) cilantro (coriander),
    coarsely chopped, plus extra for
    garnish
— 3–4 shallots, sliced
— 1 teaspoon superfine (caster) sugar
— 10 kaffir lime leaves, finely sliced
— ½ cup (1 oz/25 g) mint leaves, plus
    extra for garnish
— raw vegetables, such as pea eggplants
    (aubergines), lettuce leaves, and
    butterfly pea flowers, for serving
— basil leaves, for serving

Dry-toast the rice flour in a small pan over low heat until fragrant, 2–3 minutes. Transfer to a mortar.

Add the mango, dried fish, chili flakes, fish sauce, scallions, cilantro, 2–3 of the shallots, the sugar, kaffir lime leaves, and mint leaves to the mortar and pound with a pestle until well mixed. Garnish with mint leaves and the remaining shallot. Serve with raw or steamed vegetables and basil leaves.

Soups

The lovely thing about Thai soups, for the home cook,
is that one smart shopping expedition for basics such
as lemongrass, galangal, coconut milk, shrimp paste, fish
sauce, and cilantro (coriander) not only strengthens your
Thai kitchen, but stands you in good stead to make a handful
of fantastic soups without going shopping again. Here's the
sour-and-spicy soup you know and love, with a chicken stock
base and flecked with tamarind leaves. There's a fish soup
for every seafood lover, whether it's a fan of sea bass
or mackerel, snakehead or mullet. And each of these
is a snap to make.

Egg Tofu and Ground Pork Soup

Serves 2–3
Cook time: 25 minutes

For the egg tofu
— 1¼ cups (300 ml) soy milk
— ¼ teaspoon salt
— 3 eggs

For the soup
— 7 oz/200 g ground (minced) pork
— 1½ teaspoons Saam-gler (page 19)
— 3 tablespoons soy sauce
— 2 cups (475 ml) chicken or pork stock
— 1½ teaspoons salt
— 2 stalks celery, chopped
— 1 bunch cilantro (coriander), leaves
  only, coarsely chopped, for garnish

To make the egg tofu, stir together the soy milk and salt in a bowl. Add the eggs and use a fork or whisk to beat the eggs and milk together very gently. Try to avoid creating bubbles. Pour the mixture into a shallow dish to a depth of 1½ inches/4 cm. Put the dish in a steamer and steam over very low heat for 12–15 minutes, until cooked and firm. Remove and cut into 1¼-inch/3 cm squares. (The egg tofu can be stored in an airtight container in the refrigerator for 2–3 days.)

To make the soup, mix together the pork and saam-gler in a large bowl. Add 1 tablespoon of the soy sauce and mix again. Shape the mixture into 20 small balls, then place on a plate and set aside.

Bring the stock and 2 cups (475 ml) water to a boil in a large pan over medium heat. Add the meatballs, reduce the heat slightly, and simmer for 2–3 minutes, until the meatballs float to the surface. Stir in the salt and remaining 2 tablespoons soy sauce, then add the egg tofu and celery. Increase the heat to medium and cook for another 2 minutes. Ladle into soup bowls, garnish with cilantro, and serve.

Mullet Soup

Serves 4
Cook time: 25 minutes

— 2¾-inch/7 cm piece fresh ginger,
peeled and sliced
— 3-inch/8 cm piece galangal,
peeled and sliced
— 1½ stalks lemongrass, sliced
— 4–5 fresh red bird's eye chilis,
finely chopped
— 2 shallots, thinly sliced
— 1 lb 2 oz/500 g gray mullet or red
snapper, cut into 2-inch/5 cm pieces
— ⅓ cup (75 ml) mangrove palm vinegar,
white vinegar, or Tamarind Puree
(page 32)
— ½ teaspoon salt

Bring 4 cups (950 ml) water to a boil in a large pan. Add the ginger, galangal, lemongrass, chilis, and shallots, return to a boil, and cook for 5 minutes. Carefully add the fish and cook for another 5 minutes. Season with the vinegar and salt. Ladle into soup bowls and serve.

Sweet and Sour Mackerel Soup

Serves 2–3
Cook time: 20 minutes

— 3 cilantro (coriander) roots*, chopped
— ½ teaspoon salt
— 1 teaspoon shrimp paste
— 4 shallots, chopped
— 3½ cups (800 ml) fish stock or water
— 4 tablespoons Tamarind Puree
  (page 32)
— 1 tablespoon granulated sugar
— 1 tablespoon fish sauce
— 5 small whole mackerels
— 1-inch/3 cm piece fresh ginger, peeled
  and julienned
— ¼ cup (1 oz/25 g) chopped scallions
  (spring onions)
— 5 fresh red bird's eye chilis, sliced
  on an angle

* *If you can't find cilantro with the
   roots still attached, just use the stems
   and double the quantity called for.*

Pound the cilantro roots, salt, shrimp paste, and shallots together in a mortar with a pestle until it forms a smooth paste. (Alternatively, combine the ingredients in a food processor and pulse to form a smooth paste.)

Bring the stock or water to a boil in a large pan over medium heat. Add the pounded mixture, stir, and return to a boil. Add the tamarind, sugar, and fish sauce and return to a boil. Add the mackerel and cook for about 10 minutes. Add the ginger and scallions and stir. Ladle into soup bowls, sprinkle with the dried chilis, and serve.

Sea Bass Soup with Cardamom Shoots

Serves 4
Cook time: 20 minutes

— 1 lb 2 oz/500 g sea bass fillets, cut into
1½-inch/4 cm pieces
— 7 oz/200 g Siam cardamom shoots*,
cut into 1½-inch/4 cm lengths
— 7 oz/200 g salacca (snake fruit),
peeled, or 1¼-inch/3 cm cubes
fresh pineapple
— 2–3 kaffir lime leaves, torn
— 1 tablespoon fish sauce
— 1 teaspoon fresh lime juice
— 3–5 fresh green bird's eye chilis,
chopped
— 1 small handful of cilantro (coriander),
chopped

* *If you can't find cardamom shoots,*
substitute bamboo shoots and
2 green cardamom pods. Add
the cardamom pods to the water
when you bring it to a boil.

Bring 4 cups (950 ml) water to a boil over medium heat. Add the sea bass, cardamom shoots, and salacca. Return to a boil and add the pineapple (if using), kaffir lime leaves, fish sauce, lime juice, chilis, and cilantro and cook for 3–4 minutes. Ladle into soup bowls and serve.

Sea Bass in Herb Soup

Serves 2
Cook time: 20 minutes

— 2 tablespoons fish sauce
— ½ tablespoon shrimp paste
— 4 shallots, chopped
— 3 cloves garlic, chopped
— 2 tablespoons Tamarind Puree
  (page 32)
— 1 teaspoon jaggery, palm sugar,
  or light brown sugar
— 1 lb 2 oz/500 g sea bass fillets,
  cut into bite-size chunks
— 20 sweet basil leaves
— 20 star gooseberry leaves
— 20 holy basil leaves

Bring 2 cups (475 ml) water to a boil in a large pan. Add the fish sauce, shrimp paste, shallots, and garlic and return to a boil. Add the tamarind and sugar and return to a boil. Add the sea bass and cook for 3–5 minutes. Remove from the heat and add the sweet basil, star gooseberry, and holy basil leaves. Ladle into soup bowls and serve.

Spicy Snakehead Fish and Lotus Stem Soup

Serves 6–8
Cook time: 20 minutes

— 3 stalks lemongrass, cut into 1-inch/3 cm pieces
— 4–5 slices galangal or ginger
— 6 kaffir lime leaves
— 3–5 shallots, sliced
— 2 tablespoons s Puree (page 32)
— 1 teaspoon salt
— 1¾ lb/800 g snakehead fish or catfish fillets, cut into 1-inch/3 cm pieces
— 2 cups (7 oz/200 g) lotus stem or root, peeled and cut into 1-inch/3 cm lengths
— 2 tablespoons fish sauce
— 2 tablespoons fresh lemon juice
— 4–5 dried red chilis, seeded and chopped
— 2 sprigs cilantro (coriander), chopped, for garnish

Bring 4 cups (950 ml) water to a boil in a large pan over medium heat. Add the lemongrass, galangal, kaffir lime leaves, shallots, tamarind, and salt and bring to a boil. Add the fish and lotus stem and cook for 8 minutes. Remove from the heat and add the fish sauce, lemon juice, and chilis. Ladle into soup bowls, garnish with the cilantro, and serve.

Spicy Shrimp Soup

Serves 6
Cook time: 20 minutes

— 2 cups (475 ml) chicken stock
— 1 teaspoon salt
— 10 thin slices galangal or ginger
— 4 kaffir lime leaves, torn
— 5–7 stalks lemongrass, sliced on an
   angle into 1¼-inch/3 cm lengths
— ½ onion, thinly sliced
— 2 plum tomatoes, quartered
— 5 oz/150 g straw or white mushrooms,
   halved
— 12 raw jumbo shrimp (king prawns),
   peeled and deveined
— 3 tablespoons fresh lime juice
— 5 fresh green bird's eye chilis, crushed
— ¼ teaspoon granulated sugar
— 2 tablespoons fish sauce
— 3 small shallots, crushed
— 3 scallions (spring onions), cut into
   1½-inch/4 cm lengths
— handful of cilantro (coriander),
   chopped

Combine the chicken stock, 2 cups (475 ml) water, and salt in a large pan. Bring to a boil over medium heat. Add the galangal, kaffir lime leaves, and lemongrass, return to a boil, and cook for 1–2 minutes. Add the onion and tomatoes, return to a boil, and add the mushrooms and shrimp. Boil for 1 minute, or until the shrimp are cooked. Add the lime juice, chilis, sugar, fish sauce, and shallots and stir. Ladle into soup bowls, sprinkle with the scallions and cilantro, and serve.

Melinjo Leaf and Shrimp in Coconut Milk Soup

Serves 2
Cook time: 10 minutes

— 2 cups (475 ml) coconut milk
— 1 tablespoon shrimp paste
— 1 teaspoon granulated sugar
— ½ teaspoon salt
— handful of melinjo leaves or baby spinach
— 4–5 raw shrimp (prawns), peeled and deveined, tails still intact

Bring the coconut milk to a boil in a large pan. Add the shrimp paste, sugar, and salt, then stir and return to a boil. Add the melinjo leaves and shrimp, bring to a boil, then reduce the heat and simmer for 2 minutes, or until the shrimp are cooked. Ladle into soup bowls and serve.

Chicken and Coconut Soup

Serves 4–6
Cook time: 25 minutes

— 3½ cups (800 ml) chicken stock
— ½ teaspoon salt
— 1 cilantro (coriander) root*
— 1 shallot, halved
— 2 stalk lemongrass, sliced on an angle
— 6 thin slices galangal or ginger
— 4 kaffir lime leaves, torn
— 11 oz/300 g boneless chicken breast
   or thigh, cut into 1¼ × 1½-inch/
   3 × 4 cm pieces
— ½ cup (4 oz/100 g) young coconut flesh
   (from inside a young coconut)
— 1½ tablespoons fish sauce
— 2½ teaspoons fresh lime juice
— ½ teaspoon granulated sugar
— scant 1 cup (200 ml) coconut milk
— 1–2 fresh red bird's eye chilis,
   chopped
— ¼ cup (0.25 oz/10 g) chopped cilantro
— 2 young coconuts, cut open at the top
   and drained (keep the tops as lids)
— 1 teaspoon Chili Jam (page 12),
   for garnish
— 4 dried red bird's eye chilis, seeded,
   for garnish

* *If you can't find cilantro with the
   roots still attached, just use the stems
   and double the quantity called for.*

Combine the chicken stock and salt in a large pan and bring to a boil over medium heat.

Pound the cilantro root, shallot, lemongrass, galangal, and kaffir leaves in a mortar with a pestle. (Alternatively, combine the ingredients in a food processor and pulse to form a smooth paste.) Add the mixture to the pan of stock and boil for 1–2 minutes. Add the chicken and boil for 3–4 minutes, until the chicken is cooked. Stir in the coconut flesh, fish sauce, lime juice, sugar, and coconut milk and cook for another 2 minutes. Add the fresh chilis and chopped cilantro, then ladle into the whole young coconuts, garnish with the chili jam and dried chilis, and serve.

Sour and Spicy Chicken Soup with Tamarind Leaves

Serves 4
Cook time: 30 minutes

— 4 cups (950 ml) chicken stock
— ½ teaspoon salt
— 5 thin slices galangal or ginger
— 2 stalks lemongrass, cut on an angle
　into 1½-inch/4 cm lengths
— 3 small shallots, lightly crushed
— 7 oz/200 g bone-in chicken, chopped
　into small pieces
— 2 tablespoons fish sauce
— 4 kaffir lime leaves, torn
— handful of young tamarind leaves or
　1 cup pickled young tamarind leaves
— 2 tomatoes, cut into wedges
— 5 fresh red bird's eye chilis, lightly
　pounded

Combine the stock and salt in a large pan and bring to a boil over high heat. Add the galangal, lemongrass, and shallots and boil for 1 minute. Add the chicken and return to a boil. Skim off any scum. Reduce the heat and simmer for 15–20 minutes, until cooked and tender. Add the fish sauce, kaffir lime leaves, tamarind leaves, tomatoes, and chilis. Ladle into soup bowls and serve.

Curries

Stock up on coconut milk. The ingredient is especially
beloved in Southern Thailand, where coconuts—and the
monkeys trained to pick them—are a major feature of rural
life. It makes several cameos in these knockout-tasty curries.
You'll see a curry for every appetite: pork with cardamom, the
roasted duck curry common in Southern Thailand, chicken
with eggplant, crab with betel leaves, and even a pescatarian-
friendly mushroom curry, bright with sweet basil and bird's
eye chilis.

Spicy Catfish and Tree Basil Curry

Serves 3–4
Cook time: 20 minutes

— 2 tablespoons vegetable oil
— 2 tablespoons Southern Chili Paste
  (page 18)
— 1⅔ cups (400 ml) coconut milk
— 1 lb 2 oz/500 g catfish, head removed,
  cut into ¾-inch/2 cm chunks
— 1 fresh green bird's eye chili, sliced
  on an angle
— 1 fresh red bird's eye chili, sliced
  on an angle
— 1½ teaspoons fish sauce
— ½ teaspoon granulated sugar
— 2 handfuls of tree basil or holy basil
  leaves, chopped
— salt

Heat the oil in a wok over medium heat. Add the chili paste, and cook for 1–2 minutes, until fragrant. Add the coconut milk and bring to a boil. Add the fish, cook for 4 minutes, then add the chilis, fish sauce, sugar, and a pinch of salt. Stir and cook for another 1–2 minutes, until the fish is fully flavored. Add the tree basil, stir a couple of times, then serve.

Dry Fish Fried with Curry

Serves 8
Cook time: 25 minutes, plus soaking time

For the chili paste
— 1 oz/20 g dried red chilis, chopped
— 1 shallot, chopped
— 1 large clove garlic, chopped
— 1 teaspoon peeled and chopped
galangal or ginger
— 1 tablespoon chopped fingerroot
or ginger
— 1 tablespoon chopped lemongrass
— 1 tablespoon shrimp paste
— 1 teaspoon salt

For the curry
— 2 lb 4 oz/1 kg whisker sheatfish,
red snapper, or red mullet, cleaned
and tails removed
— 4 cups (950 ml) vegetable oil, for
deep-frying, plus ¼ cup (60 ml)
— 2 tablespoons fish sauce
— 1 tablespoon granulated sugar
— 1 teaspoon ground white pepper
— grated zest of ½ kaffir lime or lime, for
garnish

To make the chili paste, soak the dried chilis in a bowl of warm water for 15 minutes or until rehydrated, then drain and chop.

Pound the chilis, shallot, garlic, galangal, fingerroot, and lemongrass in a mortar with a pestle until smooth. (Alternatively, combine the ingredients in a food processor and pulse to form a smooth paste.) Add the shrimp paste and salt and pound (or pulse) again until thoroughly combined. Set aside.

To make the curry, cut each fish into 3 pieces crosswise. Heat the 4 cups (950 ml) oil in a wok or deep-fryer to 340°F/170°C or until a cube of bread browns in 30 seconds. Deep-fry the fish for about 7 minutes, or until golden brown and crispy. Remove with a slotted spoon and drain on paper towels.

Heat the remaining ¼ cup (60 ml) oil in a pan over medium heat. Add the chili paste and stir-fry for about 3 minutes, or until fragrant. Carefully pour in ½ cup (120 ml) water, then stir in the fish sauce, sugar, and white pepper. Add the deep-fried fish, stir, and cook for another 3–4 minutes. Garnish with the lime zest and serve.

ขนมจีนน้ำยา

Spicy Fish Ball Curry with Rice Vermicelli

Serves 5
Cook time: 20 minutes, plus soaking time

For the chili paste
— 5–8 dried red chilis, seeded
— 1 teaspoon salt
— 1½ teaspoons chopped lemongrass
— 2 teaspoons chopped galangal
  or ginger
— 2 shallots, chopped
— 3 cloves garlic, coarsely chopped
— 1½ teaspoons finely chopped fresh
  turmeric root or ½ teaspoon ground
  turmeric

For the curry
— 2 tablespoons shrimp paste
— 1 cup (5 oz/150 g) cooked fish
— 2 cups (475 ml) coconut milk
— 5 oz/150 g fish balls
— 4 tablespoons fish sauce
— 2 tablespoons jaggery, palm sugar,
  or light brown sugar
— 2 dried garcinia or 1 tablespoon
  Tamarind Puree (page 32)
— ½ cup (120 ml) coconut cream
— 1 lb 12 oz/800 g cooked rice vermicelli
— hard-boiled eggs, for garnish
— raw or steamed vegetables, such as
  beans, sprouts, lettuce, and cucumbers

To make the chili paste, soak the dried chilis in a bowl of warm water for 15 minutes or until rehydrated, then drain and chop. Pound the chilis, salt, lemongrass, galangal, shallots, garlic, and turmeric together in a mortar with a pestle until smooth. (Alternatively, combine the ingredients in a food processor and pulse to form smooth paste.)

To make the curry, add the shrimp paste and cooked fish to the chili paste and pound (or pulse) to a paste.

Heat the coconut milk in a pan over medium-low heat. Add the pounded fish mixture, stir, and bring to a boil. Boil for 3–4 minutes, then add the fish balls and season with the fish sauce, sugar, and dried garcinia or tamarind. Reduce the heat to low, then add the coconut cream and simmer for 3 minutes. Remove from the heat and transfer the curry to a large serving bowl.

Place the rice vermicelli on a serving plate and garnish with hard-boiled eggs. Serve with the spicy curry and raw or steamed vegetables.

Crab Curry with Betel Leaves

Serves 2
Cook time: 25 minutes, plus soaking time

For the red curry paste
— 3 large dried red chilis
— 5 dried bird's eye chilis
— 1 cilantro (coriander) root*
— 1 tablespoon thinly sliced lemongrass
— 1 tablespoon sliced galangal or ginger
— 2 shallots, chopped
— 2 cloves garlic
— ¾ teaspoon thinly sliced kaffir lime zest
— salt and ground white pepper
— 1½ tablespoons ground black pepper
— ½ teaspoon cumin seeds, dry-toasted
— ½ teaspoon coriander seeds, dry-toasted
— 2 teaspoons chopped fresh turmeric
— ¼ teaspoon shrimp paste

For the curry
— 14 oz/400 g dried rice vermicelli
— 2 tablespoons vegetable oil
— 2 cups (475 ml) coconut milk
— 1½ teaspoons fish sauce
— 1½ teaspoons jaggery, palm sugar,
  or light brown sugar
— 2 kaffir lime leaves
— 4 oz/100 g betel, thinly sliced, plus
  10 whole betel leaves for serving
— 9 oz/250 g crabmeat
— 10 cilantro leaves
— 1 red spur chili, seeded and slivered

To make the curry paste, soak the dried chilis in warm water for 15 minutes; drain and chop. Pound the chilis and the remaining paste ingredients in a mortar with a pestle until smooth. (Or, pulse the ingredients in a food processor.)

Meanwhile, for the curry, soak the vermicelli in water for 5 minutes. Drain. Bring a pan with water to a boil, add the vermicelli, and cook for 1–2 minutes. Rinse under cold water and drain.

Heat the oil in a pan over medium heat, add 3 tablespoons of the curry paste, and stir-fry for 1–2 minutes. Pour in the coconut milk and bring to a boil. Stir in the fish sauce, sugar, lime leaves, and sliced betel leaves and cook for 1–2 minutes. Add the crabmeat and gently stir for 1 minute.

Use your hands to roll the vermicelli into 10 small rolls. Place each roll on a whole betel leaf and top with a cilantro leaf and 2 slivers of chili. Ladle the curry into bowls and serve with vermicelli-topped betel leaves.

* *If you can't find cilantro with the roots still attached, just use the stems and double the quantity called for.*

Fish Curry with Fermented Rice Noodles

Serves 6
Cook time: 30 minutes

— 1 lb 8 oz/700 g snakehead fish, catfish,
  or sea bass fillet
— 3 tablespoons Southern Chili Paste
  (page 18)
— 4¼ cups (1 liter) coconut milk
— 3½ tablespoons fish sauce
— 4 kaffir lime leaves, torn
— ½ teaspoon granulated sugar

For serving
— 2 lb 4 oz/1 kg cooked fermented rice
  noodles or rice noodles
— 1 cup (4 oz/100 g) bean sprouts
— 3 cups (11 oz/300 g) thinly sliced
  yard-long beans or green beans
— 1 stalk lemongrass, thinly sliced
— 1 cucumber, sliced

Put the fish in a steamer and steam for
5–7 minutes, until cooked. Remove from the
steamer and remove and discard the skin.

Pound the fish and chili paste in a mortar with
a pestle until combined. Set aside.

Bring the coconut milk to a boil in a large pan
over medium heat. Add the chili paste mixture and
stir until thoroughly combined. Return to a boil,
then reduce the heat to low and simmer for about
2 minutes. Stir in the fish sauce, kaffir leaves, and
sugar and simmer for another 5 minutes, or until
full-flavored. Remove from the heat and set aside.

To serve, divide the noodles among serving bowls
and pour ¾ cup (175 ml) of the curry into each
bowl. Top with the bean sprouts, yard-long beans,
lemongrass, and cucumber and serve.

Pork Curry with Siam Cardamom Shoots

Serves 2
Cook time: 25 minutes, plus soaking time

— 2 cups (5 oz/150 g) thinly sliced
  Siam cardamom shoots*
— 1⅔ cups (400 ml) coconut milk
— 3 tablespoons Southern Chili Paste
  (page 18)
— 11 oz/300 g pork tenderloin (fillet)
  or boneless loin chops (steaks),
  thinly sliced
— 1½ teaspoons fish sauce
— ½ teaspoon salt
— ½ teaspoon granulated sugar
— 5 kaffir lime leaves, torn
— Steamed Jasmine Rice (page 204),
  for serving

* *If you can't find cardamom shoots, use*
  an equal amount of bamboo shoots
  and 4 green cardamom pods. Add
  the cardamom pods to the coconut
  milk when you bring it to a boil.

Soak the cardamom shoots in a bowl of water for 1–2 minutes, then drain and set aside.

Bring half the coconut milk to a boil in a pan over medium heat. Add the chili paste and stir for 4–5 minutes, until fragrant and the coconut milk has thickened. Add the pork and cardamom shoots and cook for about 5 minutes or until the pork is cooked. Add the remaining coconut milk and season with the fish sauce, salt, sugar, and kaffir lime leaves. Return to a boil and cook for 3–4 minutes. Serve with rice.

Roasted Duck Curry with Lychee

Serves 4
Cook time: 30 minutes, plus
marinating time

— 14 oz/400 g skin-on duck breast
— 1 tablespoon soy sauce
— 3 tablespoons vegetable oil
— 2½ tablespoons Red Curry Paste
  (page 16)
— 1⅔ cups (400 ml) coconut milk
— scant ½ cup (100 ml) chicken stock
— 2½ tablespoons fish sauce
— 2½ tablespoons jaggery, palm sugar,
  or light brown sugar
— 2–3 round eggplants (aubergines),
  quartered
— scant 1 cup (4 oz/100 g) pea eggplants
  (aubergines)
— ⅔ cup (4 oz/100 g) fresh pineapple
  cubes (1¼ inch/3 cm)
— 5–6 kaffir lime leaves, torn
— 10 lychees or rambutans, peeled and
  pitted
— Steamed Jasmine Rice (page 204),
  for serving
— Thai basil leaves, for garnish
— 1 fresh red bird's eye chili, finely
  sliced, for garnish

Put the duck breast in a shallow dish and rub the soy sauce all over the meat, then let marinate for 5–10 minutes.

Preheat the broiler (grill) to high. Place the duck breast on the broiler rack and broil for 7–8 minutes on each side, until the skin is browned. Remove and slice the duck into pieces ⅝ inch/1½ cm thick. Set aside.

Heat the oil in a wok over medium heat. Add the curry paste and sauté for 1–2 minutes, until sizzling and fragrant. Pour in the coconut milk, bring to a boil, and boil for 2–3 minutes. Add the duck and stock and boil for another 3–4 minutes, then add the fish sauce, sugar, eggplants, pineapple, kaffir lime leaves, and lychees. Boil for another 4–5 minutes.

Serve with rice and garnish with basil leaves and red chili.

Chicken Curry with Herbs

Serves 6
Cook time: 30 minutes

— 3 tablespoons vegetable oil
— 3 tablespoons Red Curry Paste
  (page 16)
— 1 lb 8 oz/700 g boneless chicken
  thigh, cut into small pieces
— 1 teaspoon salt
— 1 cup (3 oz/80 g) chopped Siam
  cardamom shoots*
— 1 cup (2 ½ oz/65 g) pea eggplants
  (aubergines), or diced round eggplants
— ½ tablespoon chopped kaffir lime
  leaves
— 1 fresh green bird's eye chili, sliced on
  an angle
— 1 fresh red bird's eye chili, sliced on
  an angle
— Steamed Jasmine Rice (page 204),
  for serving

* *If you can't find cardamom shoots, use
   an equal amount of bamboo shoots
   and the seeds from 2 cardamom
   pods. Add the cardamom seeds
   when you add the eggplants.*

Heat the oil in a wok over medium heat.
Add the curry paste and sauté for 1 minute,
or until fragrant. Add the chicken and stir-
fry for 4–5 minutes. Carefully pour in ½ cup
(120 ml) water and cook for another 10 minutes,
or until the chicken is cooked. Season with the
salt. Add the cardamom shoots and eggplants
and cook for 2 minutes, then add the kaffir lime
leaves and chilis and cook for 2 minutes.

Fill a small bowl to the rim with the rice and turn
upside down in the middle of a serving plate.
Serve with the curry.

Spicy Chicken Curry with Bamboo Shoots

Serves 2
Cook time: 25 minutes

— 4–5 fresh orange and red bird's eye
  chilis, chopped
— 4–5 cloves garlic, chopped
— 2 tablespoons vegetable oil
— 7 oz/200 g boneless, skinless chicken
  breast, cut into bite-size pieces
— 2¼ cups (11 oz/300 g) sliced bamboo
  shoots
— 2 tablespoons fish sauce
— 1 teaspoon granulated sugar
— 4–5 kaffir lime leaves, torn
— handful of holy basil or sweet basil
  leaves, for granish
— 1 fresh red bird's eye chili, sliced on
  an angle, for garnish
— Steamed Jasmine Rice (page 204),
  for serving

Pound the chilis and garlic together in a mortar with a pestle until smooth.

Heat the oil in a wok over medium heat. Add the chili-garlic mixture and sauté for 1 minute, or until fragrant. Add the chicken and stir-fry for 3–4 minutes, until the chicken is cooked. Add the bamboo shoots and stir-fry for another 1 minute. Season with the fish sauce, sugar, and kaffir lime leaves and stir-fry for 3–4 minutes until thoroughly combined. Garnish with the basil leaves and sliced chili, and serve with rice.

Steamed Mushroom Curry in Banana Leaves

Serves 2
Cook time: 30 minutes

— 5 oz/150 g mushrooms, such as
   white beech or hoshimeji, cleaned
   and stems trimmed
— 2 tablespoons beaten egg
— 1 stalk lemongrass, finely sliced
— handful of sweet basil leaves, torn
— 2–3 fresh red bird's eye chilis
— 1 shallot, sliced
— 2½ teaspoons fish sauce
— 2 banana leaf sheets, about
   8 × 9 inches/20 × 23 cm

Mix the mushrooms, egg, lemongrass, basil leaves, chilis, and shallot together in a bowl. Add the fish sauce and mix again.

Place the 2 banana leaf sheets back to back on a work surface with the shiny surface facing outward on both sides. Put the mushroom mixture in the center of the banana leaf sheets and flatten the mixture slightly to make it easy to wrap. Fold in the sides of the sheets to cover the curry, then fold over the ends and secure with a toothpick.

Steam the banana-leaf package in a steamer for 15 minutes, or until cooked. Unwrap and serve.

Grilled, Poached, and Fried

Triumph at your next barbecue and take a break from the ho-hum "salt, pepper, and olive oil" approach by throwing Thai-spiced shrimp on the barbecue. Here are all the grilled, poached, and fried seafood recipes you need, from grilled shrimp, squid, and sea bass to a deep-fried soft-shell crab bristling with garlic and oyster sauce. Although Southern Thailand is most renowned for its seafood, grilling culture is enormously popular in Bangkok and Northern Thailand—where you might see skewers of charcoal grilled fish sausages, or long threads of smoky eggplant—too.

Grilled Giant Freshwater Shrimp

Serves 4
Cook time: 10 minutes

— 2 lb 4 oz/1 kg raw giant freshwater
  shrimp (prawns), halved lengthwise
— Seafood Dipping Sauce (page 26)

Before you begin cooking, check that your charcoal is glowing white hot, or your gas grill (barbecue) is preheated to 400°F/200°C. Grill the shrimp over an indirect heat for 3–4 minutes on each side, until they turn pink and are cooked. Serve with the seafood dipping sauce.

Grilled, Poached, and Fried

Grilled Squid

Serves 2
Cook time: 20 minutes

— 14 oz/400 g squid, cleaned
— Seafood Dipping Sauce (page 26),
   for serving

Before you begin cooking, check that your charcoal is glowing white hot, or your gas grill (barbecue) is preheated to 400°F/200°C. (Alternatively, use a conventional indoor broiler [grill] preheated to high, with the rack about 4 inches/10 cm away from the heat source.)

Score 3–4 cuts across the body of the squid, making sure that you don't cut all the way through the flesh. Grill the squid over high heat for 6–7 minutes on each side, until cooked. (If using an indoor broiler, place the squid on the rack and cook for 6–7 minutes on each side, until cooked.) Remove and slice into rings. Serve with the seafood dipping sauce.

Grilled Trevally Fish

Serves 2
Cook time: 20 minutes

For the dipping sauce
— ½ cup (120 ml) Tamarind Puree
  (page 32)
— 2½ tablespoons jaggery, palm sugar,
  or light brown sugar
— 3 fresh red and green bird's eye chilis,
  chopped
— 2 shallots, finely chopped
— 1 teaspoon salt

For the fish
— 1 lb 7 oz/650 g whole trevally fish,
  kingfish, or sea bream
— ¾ teaspoon salt
— 1 banana leaf, for wrapping

For the dipping sauce, combine the tamarind and sugar in a pan and bring to a boil over medium heat, stirring until the sugar has dissolved. Let cool, then add the chilis, shallots, and salt and mix well. Set aside.

To make the fish, before you begin cooking, check that your charcoal is glowing white hot, or your gas grill (barbecue) is preheated to 350°F/180°C. (Alternatively, use a conventional indoor broiler [grill] preheated to medium with the rack about 4 inches/10 cm away from the heat source.)

Rub the fish with the salt and place in the center of the banana leaf. Fold in the sides of the leaf to cover the fish, then fold over the ends and secure with toothpicks.

Grill the fish over medium heat for 6–8 minutes on each side until cooked. (If using an indoor broiler, place the fish on the rack and cook for 7–8 minutes on each side, turning occasionally, until cooked.)

Unwrap the fish and serve with the dipping sauce on the side.

Steamed Fish with Pumpkin and Herbs

Serves 4
Cook time: 25 minutes

— 14 oz/400 g whole tilapia
— ½ teaspoon salt
— 2 shallots, chopped
— 2 cloves garlic, chopped
— 1 teaspoon black peppercorns
— 3 cilantro (coriander) roots*, chopped
— 1 tablespoon soy sauce
— 2 stalks lemongrass, halved crosswise
   and crushed
— 8 thin slices galangal or ginger
— 7 oz/200 g pumpkin wedge, cut into
   3–4 pieces
— handful of holy basil or Greek basil,
   for garnish

For serving
— Steamed Jasmine Rice (page 204)
— Seafood Dipping Sauce (page 26)

*   *If you can't find cilantro with the
    roots still attached, just use the stems
    and double the quantity called for.*

Rinse the fish in cold water, pat dry with paper towels, then rub the whole fish with the salt and set aside.

Coarsely pound the shallots, garlic, black peppercorns, and cilantro roots together in a mortar with a pestle. Add the soy sauce and stuff the mixture inside the fish cavity.

Put the lemongrass and galangal in the center of a large heatproof plate or foil packet, then place the fish on top. Arrange the pumpkin around the fish and steam in a steamer for about 15 minutes, or until the fish is cooked. Garnish with the basil and serve with rice and seafood dipping sauce.

Sweet Poached Mackerel

Serves 3
Cook time: 15 minutes

— 5 small whole mackerels
— 5 cloves garlic, smashed
— 2–3-inch/5–8 cm piece fresh ginger,
   peeled and pounded
— 2 tablespoons jaggery, palm sugar,
   or light brown sugar
— 1 tablespoon Tamarind Puree
   (page 32)
— 1 teaspoon salt

Bring a large pan of water to a boil over medium heat, then add all the ingredients, reduce the heat to low, and simmer until the fish is cooked through but still holds its shape, about 10 minutes. Serve hot or cold.

Pumpkin in Coconut Milk

Serves 6–8
Cook time: 20 minutes

— 2 lb 4 oz/1 kg Thai pumpkin or
   kabocha squash, peeled and seeded
— 6 cups (1.4 liters) coconut milk
— 1 cup (225 g) jaggery, palm sugar,
   or light brown sugar
— ¼ cup (50 g) granulated sugar
— 1 teaspoon salt
— 1¼ cups (300 ml) coconut cream

Cut the pumpkin into sticks ½ × 1 inch/1 × 3 cm.
Rinse under cold running water and transfer to
a pan.

Add the coconut milk to the pumpkin sticks and
bring to a boil over medium heat. Reduce the heat
to medium-low and simmer for about 10 minutes,
or until the pumpkin has softened. Add the sugars
and salt and return to a boil, then add the coconut
cream. Return to a boil, remove from the heat,
and serve.

Fried Sea Bass

Serves 4
Cook time: 30 minutes

— ½ cup (80 g) julienned peeled unripe green mango, unripe green papaya, or jicama
— ½ cup (50 g) julienned carrot
— 5 shallots, chopped
— 3 tablespoons fish sauce
— 2 tablespoons fresh lime juice
— 4–5 fresh red and green bird's eye chilis, chopped
— 1½ tablespoons superfine (caster) sugar
— 1 lb 2 oz/500 g whole sea bass or red snapper
— 3 cups (750 ml) vegetable oil, for deep-frying

For the topping
— 1 tablespoon fish sauce
— 1 tablespoon jaggery, palm sugar, or light brown sugar

Put the mango, carrot, shallots, fish sauce, lime juice, chopped chilis, and superfine sugar in a large bowl and mix well. Set aside.

Butterfly the fish by cutting the fish lengthwise down the middle to the backbone, without cutting all the way through, then open out to create a butterfly fillet, leaving the head and bones intact. Pat dry with paper towels.

Heat the oil in a wok or deep-fryer to 350°F/180°C or until a cube of bread browns in 30 seconds. Deep-fry the sea bass for 15 minutes, or until golden brown and crispy. Remove with a slotted spoon and drain on paper towels. Set aside 1 tablespoon of the oil.

To make the fish topping, put the fish sauce and brown sugar in a small bowl and mix until the sugar has dissolved.

Heat the reserved 1 tablespoon oil in a wok over medium heat. Add the topping mixture and heat for 1 minute, or until it starts sizzling. Pour the sizzling mixture over the fish and top with the mango-carrot mixture. Serve.

Spicy Fried Sea Bass

Serves 4
Cook time: 30 minutes

— 1 lb 5 oz/600 g whole sea bass
— 4¼ cups (1 liter) plus 2 tablespoons
   vegetable oil
— 6 cloves garlic, chopped
— 2 fresh red bird's eye chilis, chopped
— 2 tablespoons granulated sugar
— 2 tablespoons fish sauce

Place the fish on a cutting (chopping) board and using a sharp knife, score the fish 2–3 times on both sides. Set aside.

Heat the 4¼ cups (1 liter) oil in a large wok or deep-fryer (one that's big enough for the whole fish) to 350°F/180°C or until a cube of bread browns in 30 seconds. Deep-fry the sea bass for 10–12 minutes on each side until golden brown, then remove with a slotted spoon and drain on paper towels. Set aside and discard the oil.

In the same wok, heat the remaining 2 tablespoons oil over medium heat. Add the garlic, chilis, sugar, fish sauce, and 1 tablespoon water and stir-fry for 1 minute until the sugar has dissolved. Spoon into a bowl and serve with the sea bass.

Deep-Fried Sea Bass on Betel Leaves

Serves 4
Cook time: 30 minutes

— 14 oz/400 g whole sea bass, filleted, with skin still on and the whole fish bone reserved
— ½ cup (2.25 oz/60 g) all-purpose (plain) flour
— 3 cups (750 ml) vegetable oil, for deep-frying
— 1 tablespoon fish sauce
— 3 tablespoons jaggery, palm sugar, or light brown sugar
— ¼ cup (2 oz/40 g) peanuts
— 1½-inch/4 cm piece fresh ginger, peeled and cut into ½-inch/1 cm dice
— 1–2 limes, cut into ½-inch/1 cm dice
— 1 shallot, cut into ½-inch/1 cm dice
— 8 fresh bird's eye chilis, chopped
— 3 stalks lemongrass, finely sliced
— 4 tablespoons Fried Shallots (page 34)
— 20 betel leaves or shisho leaves, for serving

Cut the sea bass fillets into ¾-inch/2 cm cubes. Put the flour in a bowl, add the fish, and toss until well coated. Remove from the bowl and set the fish aside. Sprinkle the remaining flour over the fish bone and set aside.

Heat the oil in a wok or deep-fryer to 350°F/180°C or until a cube of bread browns in 30 seconds. Deep-fry the fish for 3–4 minutes, until golden brown. Drain on paper towels. Add the fish bone to the oil in the wok and fry for 3 minutes per side. Drain on paper towels.

Combine the fish sauce and sugar in a small pan and stir over medium-low heat for 2–3 minutes to dissolve the sugar. Let the sauce cool, then transfer to a large bowl. Add the peanuts, ginger, limes, shallot, chilis, and lemongrass and mix until thoroughly combined. Set aside.

Place the deep-fried fish bone on a serving plate and arrange the fish cubes on top. Pour over the peanut mixture and sprinkle with the fried shallots. To serve, wrap bite-size portions of the fish mixture in a betel leaf and eat whole.

Deep-Fried Pork and Crabmeat in Shells

Serves 4–6
Cook time: 30 minutes

— 1 lb 2 oz/500 g ground (minced) pork
— ½ cup (2 oz/65 g) finely diced canned water chestnuts
— 1 lb 2 oz/500 g crabmeat
— 2 onions, finely chopped
— 3 cilantro (coriander) roots*, finely crushed
— 2 tablespoons soy sauce
— 3 eggs
— 12 scallop shells
— 2 cups (475 ml) vegetable oil, for deep-frying
— 3 tablespoons all-purpose (plain) flour
— lettuce leaves, for serving
— Sweet Chili Dipping Sauce (page 30), for serving
— thin slivers of red, green, and orange bell peppers, for garnish

* *If you can't find cilantro with the roots still attached, just use the stems and double the quantity called for.*

Combine the pork, water chestnuts, crabmeat, and onions in a large bowl and mix well. Add the cilantro roots, soy sauce, and 1 of the eggs and mix well. Divide the seasoned pork and crabmeat mixture among the scallop shells and set up a steamer.

Heat the oil for deep-frying in a large wok or deep fryer to 350°F/180°C or until a cube of bread browns in 30 seconds.

While the oil is getting hot, steam the filled scallop shells for 10 minutes.

Beat the remaining 2 eggs with the flour in a bowl until thoroughly combined. Working in batches, dip the steamed filled shells into the batter until coated, then carefully drop into the hot oil and deep-fry for 4–6 minutes, until golden brown and crispy. Remove with a slotted spoon and drain on paper towels.

Serve with lettuce leaves and sweet chili dipping sauce. Garnish with the pepper slivers.

Grilled, Poached, and Fried

Deep-Fried Soft-Shell Crab with Garlic

Serves 2
Cook time: 25 minutes

— 4 cups (950 ml) vegetable oil
— 10 cloves garlic, unpeeled and chopped
— 1 tablespoon Saam-gler (page 19)
— 3 tablespoons oyster sauce
— 1 tablespoon superfine (caster) sugar
— 4 soft-shell crabs (4 oz/100 g each), cleaned and cut into quarters
— lettuce leaves, for serving
— Sweet Chili Dipping Sauce (page 30), for serving

Heat ⅓ cup (75 ml) of the oil in a wok over medium-low heat. Add the garlic and fry for 1 minute, or until browned and crispy. Remove with a slotted spoon and drain on paper towels.

Put the saam-gler, oyster sauce, and sugar in a large bowl and mix well until combined. Add the crabs and gently mix.

Heat the remaining 3⅔ cups (875 ml) oil in a clean wok or deep-fryer to 350°F/180°C or until a cube of bread browns in 30 seconds. Deep-fry the crabs for 8–10 minutes, until golden brown and crispy. Remove with a slotted spoon and drain on paper towels.

Place the crab on a bed of lettuce leaves, sprinkle with the crispy garlic, and serve with sweet chili dipping sauce.

Deep-Fried Shrimp

Serves 2
Cook time: 15 minutes

— ½ cup (60 g) all-purpose (plain) flour
— ¼ cup (80 g) rice flour
— ½ cup (60 g) tapioca flour
— ¼ teaspoon baking powder
— ¼ teaspoon salt
— 1 cup (50 g) fresh breadcrumbs or panko breadcrumbs
— 9 oz/250 g raw shrimp (prawns), peeled and deveined, with tails still intact
— 3 cups (750 ml) vegetable oil, for deep-frying
— Sweet Chili Dipping Sauce (page 30), for serving

Put the all-purpose flour, rice flour, tapioca flour, baking powder, salt, and 1 cup (235 ml) water in a large bowl and mix well until the flours have dissolved. Set aside.

Spread the breadcrumbs out on a plate. Dip the shrimp into the flour mixture, then coat in the breadcrumbs.

Heat the oil in a wok or deep-fryer to 350°F/ 180°C or until a cube of bread browns in 30 seconds. Working in batches, deep-fry the shrimp for 4–5 minutes, until golden brown. Remove with a slotted spoon and drain on paper towels. Serve with the sweet chili dipping sauce.

Pork Floss Wrapped in Kale Leaves

Makes 10
Cook time: 15 minutes

For the sweet and sour dressing
— 2½ tablespoons jaggery, palm sugar,
   or light brown sugar
— 1 tablespoon fish sauce
— 1 tablespoon fresh lime juice
— 1½ teaspoons pickled plum juice
   (optional)

For the pork
— 1-inch/3 cm piece fresh ginger, peeled
   and cut into ½-inch/1 cm dice
— 6 fresh red and green bird's eye chilis,
   finely chopped
— 2 shallots, finely chopped
— 2 stalks lemongrass, finely sliced
— 3 tablespoons roasted peanuts
— 1 lime, cut into ½-inch/1 cm dice
— 2 oz/50 g pork floss
— 20 young Chinese kale leaves

To make the dressing, mix together the sugar, fish sauce, lime juice, and pickled plum juice (if using) in a pan and stir over medium heat for about 2 minutes, or until the sugar has dissolved and starts to caramelize. Let cool.

To make the pork, mix together the ginger, chilis, shallots, lemongrass, roasted peanuts, lime, pork floss, and the dressing in a large bowl.

To serve, place the kale leaves on a serving plate and put 1½ tablespoons of the pork mixture into the center of each leaf.

Stir-Fries

Thai cooks understand the flavors you want from a stir-fry and how to make them boom quickly and with few ingredients. Invest in an inexpensive wok, whose benefits are numerous: Because of its shape, you can maneuver ingredients easily, and keep your stovetop cleaner than you would with a deep Dutch oven or skillet. (Grease tends to stay within a wok's confines.) Here is stir-fried kale with the salted fish known and loved in Northeast Thailand. There is the beef with broccoli in oyster sauce—ready in 15 minutes!—plus the phat Thai (one of Thailand's most recognized dishes), ready in 30.

เต้าหู้ผัดถั่วงอก

Stir-Fried Tofu with Bean Sprouts

Serves 2
Cook time: 15 minutes

— 1 cup (250 ml) vegetable oil
— 4 oz/100 g extra-firm tofu, cut into
   ¾-inch/2 cm cubes
— 5 cloves garlic, finely chopped
— 3 cups (11 oz/300 g) bean sprouts
— 3 fresh red bird's eye chilis, sliced
   on an angle
— 2 scallions (spring onions), cut into
   1¼-inch/3 cm lengths
— 2 tablespoons oyster sauce
— 1 teaspoon soy sauce

Heat the oil in a wok over medium heat. Add the tofu and stir-fry for 4–5 minutes, until golden. Remove with a slotted spoon and set aside. Drain all but 2 tablespoons of the oil from the wok. Increase the heat to medium-high and heat the oil. Add the garlic and bean sprouts and stir-fry for 1–2 minutes. Add the chilis, scallions, oyster sauce, soy sauce, and tofu and stir-fry for another 1 minute. Serve.

Stir-Fried Sea Bass with Cardamom Shoots

Serves 2
Cook time: 15 minutes

— 3–5 fresh orange finger chilis, chopped
— 5–10 cloves garlic, chopped
— 3 tablespoons vegetable oil
— 11 oz/300 g sea bass fillet, cut into
  ½-inch/1 cm pieces
— 1½ tablespoons fish sauce
— 1 cup (4 oz/120 g) chopped Siam
  cardamom shoots*
— 1 cup (2 oz/50 g) holy basil leaves,
  plus extra for serving

* *If you can't find cardamom shoots,
use an equal amount of bamboo
shoots and ¼ teaspoon cardamom
seeds. Add the cardamom seeds when
you stir-fry the chili-garlic paste.*

Pound the chilis and garlic together in a mortar with a pestle until smooth.

Heat the oil in a wok over medium heat. Add the paste and stir-fry for 1 minute, or until fragrant. Add the sea bass and fish sauce and cook for 3–5 minutes. Add the cardamom shoots and basil and cook for another 2 minutes. Serve with extra basil.

Stir-Fried Kale with Salted Fish

Serves 2
Cook time: 15 minutes

— 2 tablespoons vegetable oil
— 2 tablespoons Fried Garlic (page 33)
— 2 fresh red bird's eye chilis, chopped
   and pounded
— 4 oz/100 g salted fish (such as Spanish
   mackerel), rinsed, dried,
   and cut into bite-size pieces
— 5–7 Chinese kale stalks, chopped
— 1 teaspoon oyster sauce
— ½ teaspoon superfine (caster) sugar

Heat the oil in a wok over medium heat. Add the fried garlic, chilis, and fish. Then add the kale and stir-fry for about 4 minutes, or until cooked. Add the oyster sauce and sugar and serve.

Stir-Fried Mushrooms, Baby Corn, and Shrimp

Serves 2
Cook time: 20 minutes

— 2 tablespoons vegetable oil
— 2–3 cloves garlic, chopped
— 8–10 raw shrimp (prawns), peeled and deveined, with tails still intact
— 14 baby corn, sliced on an angle into 1½-inch/ 4 cm lengths
— 4 oz/100 g termite or shiitake mushrooms, sliced
— 1 teaspoon soy sauce
— 2 tablespoons oyster sauce
— ½ teaspoon superfine (caster) sugar
— 1 scallion (spring onion), sliced into 1¼-inch/ 3 cm lengths

Heat the oil in a wok over medium-high heat. Add the garlic and stir-fry for 30 seconds, or until fragrant. Add the shrimp and stir-fry for 1 minute, or until cooked. Remove and set aside.

Add the baby corn to the wok and stir-fry for 2–3 minutes, until softened. While stir-frying, add ¼ cup (60 ml) water. Add the mushrooms, stir-fry for another 1 minute, then return the shrimp to the wok. Add the soy sauce, oyster sauce, sugar, and scallion and stir-fry for 30 seconds. Serve.

Stir-Fried Squid

Serves 4
Cook time: 20 minutes

— 5 cloves garlic
— 2 shallots, chopped
— 5 teaspoons shrimp paste
— ¼ teaspoon ground white pepper
— 3 tablespoons vegetable oil
— 14 oz/400 g squid, cleaned and sliced
  into rings ½ inch/1 cm thick, tentacles
  reserved
— 5 scallions (spring onions), white
  and light green part only, cut into
  1 ¼-inch/3 cm lengths
— 1½ tablespoons oyster sauce
— 1 tablespoon fish sauce
— 1 teaspoon granulated sugar
— 1 tablespoon small pickled garlic
  cloves
— lettuce leaves, for serving

Pound the garlic, shallots, shrimp paste, and white pepper in a mortar with a pestle until a smooth paste.

Heat the oil in a wok over medium heat. Add the paste and stir-fry for 1 minute, or until fragrant. Increase the heat to medium-high, add the squid rings and tentacles, and stir-fry for another 5 minutes. Add the scallions, oyster sauce, fish sauce, and sugar and mix well. Add the pickled garlic and stir-fry for another 30 seconds. Serve on a bed of lettuce.

Stir-Fried Beef with Broccoli in Oyster Sauce

Serves 2

Cook time: 15 minutes

— 2 tablespoons vegetable oil

— 3 cloves garlic, finely chopped

— 5 oz/150 g beef sirloin or tenderloin (fillet), cut into slices ¼ inch/5 mm thick

— 2½ tablespoons oyster sauce

— 1 tablespoon soy sauce

— 14 oz/400 g Chinese broccoli, cut into 2-inch/5 cm lengths

Heat the oil in a wok over medium heat. Add the garlic and stir-fry for 1 minute, or until fragrant. Add the beef and stir-fry for 1 minute, then season with the oyster sauce and soy sauce and stir-fry for 30 seconds. Add the broccoli and 2 tablespoons water and stir-fry for another 2 minutes or until the broccoli has softened slightly. Serve.

Stir-Fried Bok Choy, Pork, and Tofu

Serves 2
Cook time: 20 minutes

— ¼ cup (30 g) all-purpose (plain) flour
— ½ recipe egg tofu (from Egg Tofu and Ground Pork Soup, page 82), cut into slices ¾ inch/2 cm thick
— 2 cups (475 ml) plus 3 tablespoons vegetable oil
— 1 tablespoon oyster sauce
— 2½ teaspoons soy sauce
— 3 cloves garlic, finely chopped
— 5 oz/150 g ground (minced) pork
— 1 lb 2 oz/500 g bok choy (pak choi), cut into 2½-inch/6 cm lengths
— 3 tablespoons vegetable stock
— ½ teaspoon ground black pepper
— pinch of granulated sugar
— ½ cup (70 g) chopped Chinese celery (1¼-inch/3 cm lengths)
— Steamed Jasmine Rice (page 204), for serving

Spread the flour out on a plate and dredge the egg tofu in the flour until well coated. Set aside.

Heat the 2 cups (475 ml) oil in a wok or deep-fryer to 350°F/180°C or until a cube of bread browns in 30 seconds. Reduce the heat to medium, carefully add the egg tofu, and deep-fry for 4–5 minutes, until golden brown. Remove with a slotted spoon and drain on paper towels.

Combine the oyster and soy sauces in a small bowl and set aside.

Heat the remaining 3 tablespoons oil in a clean wok over medium-high heat. Add the garlic and stir-fry for 30 seconds, or until fragrant. Add the pork and stir-fry for about 1 minute or until the pork begins to brown. Add the bok choy and stir-fry for 2 minutes, then add the soy sauce mixture, stock, black pepper, sugar, and celery. Stir well, then add the egg tofu. Gently stir for another 40–50 seconds, until well mixed. Serve with rice.

ผัดไทยไร้เส้น

Phat Thai without Noodles

Serves 2
Cook time: 30 minutes

— 1 cup (250 ml) vegetable oil
— 4 oz/100 g extra-firm white or yellow
  tofu, cut into ½-inch/1 cm cubes
— 1 shallot, finely chopped
— 4 oz/100 g pork shoulder or loin, thinly
  sliced
— 2 tablespoons chopped pickled radish
— 10 raw shrimp (prawns), peeled and
  deveined, with tails still intact
— 2 eggs, beaten
— 2 tablespoons dried shrimp
— 4 teaspoons granulated sugar
— 1½ teaspoons fresh lime juice
— 1 tablespoon fish sauce
— 2–3 tablespoons roasted peanuts,
  finely pounded, plus extra for garnish
— 3 fresh red chilis, finely chopped
— ½ teaspoon dried chili flakes
— 1 cup (4 oz/100 g) bean sprouts
— 2 Chinese chives, cut into pieces
  1½ inches/4 cm long
— cilantro (coriander) sprigs, for garnish
— lime wedges, for serving

Heat the oil in a wok to 350°F/180°C or until a cube of bread browns in 30 seconds. Deep-fry the tofu for 4–5 minutes, until golden brown. Remove with a slotted spoon and drain on paper towels.

Drain all but 3 tablespoons of the oil from the wok and heat over medium heat. Add the shallot and stir-fry for 1 minute. Add the pork and stir-fry for 2–3 minutes, until cooked. Add the pickled radish and shrimp and stir-fry for another 2–3 minutes, until the shrimp are cooked.

Add the eggs and cook for 10 seconds. Add the dried shrimp and tofu and stir-fry for another 1 minute. Increase the heat a little, add the sugar, lime juice, fish sauce, roasted peanuts, fresh chilis, and chili flakes and stir-fry for 1 minute. Add the bean sprouts and chives and stir 2–3 times. Transfer to a serving dish and garnish with peanuts and cilantro sprigs. Serve with lime wedges.

Spicy Stir-Fried Pork Belly

Serves 2
Cook time: 20 minutes

— 2 tablespoons vegetable oil
— 14 oz/400 g pork belly (side) cut
   into pieces ½ inch/1 cm thick
— 2 tablespoons Red Curry Paste
   (page 16)
— 1 tablespoon jaggery, palm sugar,
   or light brown sugar
— 1 tablespoon fish sauce
— 5 kaffir lime leaves, finely sliced
— Steamed Jasmine Rice (page 204),
   for serving

Heat the oil in a wok over high heat. Add the pork and stir-fry for 6–7 minutes, until the pork is cooked and starts to brown. Remove the pork with a slotted spoon, reduce the heat to medium, and add the curry paste to the wok. Stir-fry for about 1 minute, or until fragrant. Return the pork to the wok and stir-fry for 1–2 minutes, until fully coated with the paste. Add the sugar and fish sauce and stir until the sugar has dissolved. Add the kaffir lime leaves and stir-fry for 30 seconds. Serve with rice.

Stir-Fried Chicken with Siam Cardamom Shoots

Serves 6
Cook time: 25 minutes

— 2 tablespoons vegetable oil
— 3–4 tablespoons Red Curry Paste
  (page 16)
— 7 oz/200 g holy basil leaves, pounded
— 2 lb 4 oz/1 kg skinless, boneless
  chicken, cut into small pieces
— 1 lb 2 oz/500 g pea eggplants
  (aubergines), or round green eggplants,
  diced
— 7 oz/200 g fresh red finger chilis,
  sliced into long strips
— 4 oz/100 g kaffir lime leaves, chopped
— 1 lb 2 oz/500 g Siam cardamom
  shoots*
— 2 tablespoons fish sauce

* *If you can't find cardamom shoots,*
  substitute an equal quantity of
  bamboo shoots and ½ teaspoon
  crushed cardamom seeds.

Heat the oil in a wok over medium heat. Add the curry paste, basil, and chicken, and stir-fry for about 10 minutes. Add the eggplants, chilis, kaffir lime leaves, cardamom shoots, fish sauce, and about 3 tablespoons water and cook for another 3 minutes. Serve.

Stir-Fried Ginger Chicken

Serves 2
Cook time: 25 minutes

— 3 tablespoons vegetable oil
— 3 cloves garlic, chopped
— 11 oz /300 g skinless, boneless
  chicken breast, cut into slices
  ¼ inch/6 mm thick
— 1 teaspoon soy sauce
— 2 tablespoons oyster sauce
— 1 teaspoon granulated sugar
— 4 oz/100 g Jew's ear mushrooms,
  chopped
— 2¾-inch/7 cm piece fresh ginger,
  peeled and julienned
— ½ teaspoon ground black pepper
— 1 scallion (spring onion), cut into
  1-inch/3 cm lengths
— 2 fresh red Thai chilis, sliced

Heat the oil in a wok over medium heat. Add the garlic and stir-fry for 1 minute, or until fragrant. Add the chicken and stir-fry for 4–5 minutes, until almost cooked. Add the soy sauce, oyster sauce, sugar, and mushrooms and stir-fry for 2–3 minutes, until the chicken is cooked, adding 2 tablespoons water if the sauce dries out. Add the ginger, black pepper, scallion, and chilis and stir-fry for 30 seconds. Serve.

Stir-Fried Shiitake Mushrooms

Serves 2
Cook time: 15 minutes

— 2–3 tablespoons vegetable oil
— 3 cloves garlic, finely chopped
— 9 oz/250 g shiitake mushrooms, stems trimmed, halved
— 4 tablespoons chicken stock
— 2½ tablespoons oyster sauce
— 1 teaspoon soy sauce
— 3 scallions (spring onions), cut into 1½-inch/4 cm lengths

Heat the oil in a wok over medium heat. Add the garlic and stir-fry for 1 minute, or until fragrant. Add the mushrooms and stir-fry for 2 minutes, or until cooked. Add the remaining ingredients and stir-fry for another 1 minute. Serve.

Stir-Fried Lotus Stems with Shrimp

Serves 2
Cook time: 10 minutes

— 2 tablespoons vegetable oil
— 3 cloves garlic, chopped
— 8 raw shrimp (prawns), peeled and deveined, with tails still intact
— 2 cups (9 oz/250 g) peeled and cut young lotus stems (¼-inch/6 mm lengths)
— 1 tablespoon fish sauce
— 1½ tablespoons oyster sauce
— 1 tablespoon granulated sugar
— 1 tablespoon salted soybeans
— Steamed Jasmine Rice (page 204), for serving

Heat the oil in a wok over medium heat. Add the garlic and stir-fry for 1 minute, or until fragrant. Add the shrimp and lotus stems, increase the heat, and cook for 1–2 minutes, until cooked. Stir in the fish sauce, oyster sauce, sugar, and soybeans. Serve with rice.

Stir-Fried Amaranth with Oyster Sauce

Serves 2–3
Cook time: 10 minutes

— 1 lb 2 oz/500 g amaranth
— 3 tablespoons vegetable oil
— 5 cloves garlic, finely chopped
— 2 tablespoons oyster sauce
— ½ teaspoon soy sauce

Clean the amaranth, shake off the excess water, and remove the bottom 2 inches/5 cm of the stems. Slice the remaining amaranth into 1½-inch/4 cm lengths.

Heat the oil in a wok over medium heat. Add the garlic and stir-fry for 1 minute, or until fragrant. Increase the heat to medium-high and add the amaranth, oyster sauce, and soy sauce. Stir-fry for 2–3 minutes, until the amaranth is cooked. Serve.

Stir-Fried Vegetables

Serves 2
Cook time: 15 minutes

— 2 tablespoons vegetable oil
— 2 tablespoons Fried Garlic (page 33)
— 3 stems Chinese kale, chopped
— 5 amaranth leaves, chopped
— ¼ napa (Chinese) cabbage, chopped
— 4 oz/100 g enoki mushrooms
— 2 tablespoons oyster sauce
— 1 tablespoon fish sauce
— 1½ teaspoons granulated sugar

Heat the oil in a wok over medium heat. Add the fried garlic, kale, amaranth, cabbage, and mushrooms and stir-fry for 4 minutes. Stir in the oyster sauce, fish sauce, and sugar and serve.

Rice and Noodles

Typically lighter and even easier to make than stir-fries, this section boasts two heavy-hitting hallmarks of Thai cuisine: rice and noodles. These are the flavor combinations that, like curries, bring an umami boom to the table: fried rice with pineapple, crispy rice noodles laced with herbs, noodles swimming in coconut milk dotted with shrimp. Here, too, is a super-simple recipe for the jasmine rice one sees throughout Central Thailand (often called "the rice bowl of Thailand"), Southern Thailand, and a small pocket of Northern Thailand (where sticky rice is more prevalent).

Crab Fried Rice

Serves 2
Cook time: 15 minutes

— 3 tablespoons vegetable oil
— 5 cloves garlic, finely chopped
— 1 egg, beaten
— 1 cup (175 g) Steamed Jasmine Rice (page 204)
— 4 oz/100 g crabmeat
— ½ onion, diced
— 4 tablespoons diced carrot
— ½ tomato, diced
— 2 scallions (spring onions), chopped
— 1 tablespoon soy sauce
— 1 tablespoon oyster sauce
— 1 tablespoon granulated sugar
— 2 tablespoons fish sauce
— 2 sprigs cilantro (coriander), chopped
— juice of 1 lime

For serving
— 1 cucumber, peeled and sliced
— 2 scallions (spring onions)
— lime wedges

Heat the oil in a wok over medium heat. Add the garlic and sauté for 30 seconds. Add the egg and stir until half-cooked. Increase the heat to medium-high, add the rice, crabmeat, onion, carrot, tomato, and chopped scallions and stir-fry for 2 minutes, or until cooked. Add the soy sauce, oyster sauce, and sugar and stir-fry for another 2 minutes. Transfer to a serving plate and sprinkle with the cilantro and season with the lime juice. Serve with cucumber, whole scallions, and lime wedges.

Fried Brown Rice with Shrimp

Serves 2
Cook time: 15 minutes

— 4 tablespoons vegetable oil
— 6 cloves garlic, finely chopped
— 11 oz/300 g raw shrimp (prawns),
  peeled and deveined, with tails
  still intact
— 2 eggs, beaten
— 2 cups (350 g) cooked brown rice
— 2 tablespoons diced deep-fried egg
  tofu (from Stir-Fried Bok Choy, Pork,
  and Tofu, page 166)
— 4 teaspoons granulated sugar
— 2 tablespoons soy sauce
— 2 tablespoons peas
— 2 tablespoons diced carrot
— 2 tablespoons diced onion

For garnish
— ½ Lebanese or Persian cucumber,
  peeled and sliced
— 2 teaspoons chopped cilantro
  (coriander)
— 1 scallion (spring onion), chopped
— 2 tablespoons corn kernels

Heat the oil in a wok over medium heat. Add the garlic and stir-fry for 1 minute, or until fragrant. Add the shrimp and stir-fry for 1–2 minutes, until they turn pink. Add the eggs and cook for 1 minute, or until cooked. Add the rice and stir-fry for 2 minutes. Add the tofu, sugar, and soy sauce and stir-fry for another 1 minute, or until fragrant. Add the peas, carrot, and onion and stir-fry for another 1 minute. Garnish with the cucumber, cilantro, scallion, and corn kernels and serve.

Crispy Curry Rice with Fermented Pork

Serves 4
Cook time: 30 minutes

— 2 cups (350 g) Steamed Jasmine Rice
   (page 204)
— 1 tablespoon Red Curry Paste (page 16)
— 1 egg
— ½ teaspoon salt
— 5 cups (1 liter) vegetable oil,
   for deep-frying
— 6 dried red chilis
— 3 oz/75 g pork rinds
— 7 oz/200 g fermented pork or cooked
   chorizo
— 3 shallots, sliced
— 4-inch/10 cm piece fresh ginger,
   peeled and very finely sliced
— 5 scallions (spring onions), finely
   sliced
— 1 tablespoon fresh lime juice
— 1½ teaspoons fish sauce
— ½ cup (3 oz/75 g) roasted peanuts
— green lettuce, for serving

Combine the steamed rice and curry paste in a large bowl and mix well. Break in the egg, add the salt, and knead by hand until combined. Scoop the mixture into balls using a 1-ounce (6 cm) scoop.

Heat the oil in a wok or deep-fryer to 350°F/180°C or until a cube of bread browns in 30 seconds. Deep-fry the rice balls for 7–9 minutes, until browned and crispy. Remove with a slotted spoon and drain on paper towels. Set aside.

Deep-fry the dried chilis for 10 seconds. Remove with a slotted spoon and drain on paper towels. Set aside.

Transfer the crispy rice balls to a large bowl. Break into small pieces, then add the pork rinds, fermented pork, shallots, ginger, and three-quarters of the scallions and mix until combined.

Season with the lime juice and fish sauce. Add the peanuts and fried chilis and mix again. Garnish with the remaining chopped scallions and serve with lettuce.

Thai Pork Fried Rice with Fried Eggs

Serves 4–6
Cook time: 15 minutes

— ½ cup (125 ml) vegetable oil
— 5–7 eggs
— 2 cloves garlic, chopped
— 5 oz/150 g pork loin or shoulder,
 cut into thin slices
— 3 cups (525 g) Steamed Jasmine Rice
 (page 204)
— 1½ tablespoons soy sauce
— 1 tablespoon oyster sauce
— ½ teaspoon granulated sugar
— 1 cup (3 oz/70 g) coarsely chopped
 Chinese kale
— ⅓ cup (40 g) sliced onions
— 1 tomato, cut into small wedges

For serving
— 1 cucumber, peeled and sliced
— lime wedges

Heat the oil in a wok over high heat. Fry 4–6 of the eggs, cooking them one at a time, about 2 minutes. Remove, cover to keep warm, and set aside.

Drain all but 2 tablespoons oil from the wok and reduce the heat to medium. Add the garlic and stir-fry for 1 minute, or until fragrant. Add the pork and stir-fry for 2–3 minutes, until cooked. Add the remaining egg, gently beat, and cook for 40–50 seconds, until the egg is lightly cooked. Add the rice and stir-fry for another 1 minute, or until well mixed. Season with the soy sauce, oyster sauce, and sugar and stir-fry for another 2 minutes until well combined. Add the kale, onions, and tomato wedges and stir-fry for 1–2 minutes.

To serve, place the rice on serving plates, top with a fried egg, and arrange the cucumber and lime wedges on the side.

Fried Rice with Pineapple

Serves 2
Cook time: 20 minutes

— 3 tablespoons vegetable oil
— 2 cloves garlic, sliced
— ¼ lb/120 g raw shrimp (prawns), peeled and deveined, with tails still intact
— 2½ cups (450 g) Steamed Jasmine Rice (page 204)
— 1½ tablespoons soy sauce
— 1 teaspoon granulated sugar
— 1 cup (160 g) fresh pineapple dice (¾ inch/2 cm)
— ½ cup (3 oz/75 g) roasted cashews
— 2 scallions (spring onions), thinly sliced, for garnish
— 2 lime wedges, for serving

Heat the oil in a wok over medium heat. Add the garlic and stir-fry for about 1 minute, or until fragrant. Add the shrimp and stir-fry for 1–2 minutes, until the shrimp turn pink. Remove the shrimp from the wok and set aside.

Add the steamed rice to the wok and stir for about 1 minute, or until the rice is well coated with the oil. Add the soy sauce, sugar, and shrimp and stir-fry for 1–2 minutes. Add the pineapple and cashews and cook for another 1 minute, stirring gently. Transfer to a serving bowl and garnish with the scallions. Serve with the lime wedges.

Crispy Rice Noodles

Serves 3
Cook time: 30 minutes, plus soaking time

— 11 oz/300 g dried rice noodles
— 4 cups (950 ml) vegetable oil, for
   deep-frying
— 10 kaffir lime leaves
— 4 oz/100 g dried red chilis
— 3 stalks lemongrass, finely sliced
— 2 tablespoons Tamarind Puree
   (page 32)
— 2 tablespoons dried chili flakes
— 1 teaspoon salt
— 2 tablespoons jaggery, palm sugar,
   or light brown sugar
— 4 tablespoons glucose or light honey

Soak the noodles in a bowl of water for 10 minutes, or according to package directions, until soft, then drain and set aside.

Heat the oil in a wok or deep-fryer to 350°F/ 180°C or until a cube of bread browns in 30 seconds. Working in batches, fry the rice noodles for 1 minute, then remove and drain on paper towels.

Deep-fry the kaffir lime leaves, dried chilis, and sliced lemongrass in the same oil for 30 seconds until crispy. Remove from the wok and drain on paper towels.

In a clean wok, combine the tamarind, chili flakes, salt, sugar, and glucose. Bring to a boil, stirring constantly, and boil for 5 minutes. Slowly pour the tamarind sauce over the fried rice noodles and stir until thoroughly combined. Serve.

Fried Noodles in Coconut Milk with Shrimp

Serves 2
Cook time: 20 minutes, plus soaking time

— 5 oz/150 g dried rice noodles
— 3–4 small shallots, finely chopped
— 15 dried red bird's eye chilis, seeded
— ½ teaspoon shrimp paste
— 1 cup (250 ml) coconut milk
— 1 tablespoon jaggery, palm sugar,
   or light brown sugar
— 1½ teaspoons Tamarind Puree
   (page 32)
— ¼ teaspoon salt
— black pepper
— 10 raw shrimp (prawns), peeled
   and deveined

For serving
— raw or steamed vegetables, such as
   cucumber, bean sprouts, and yard-long
   beans or green beans

Soak the noodles in a bowl of water for 10 minutes, or according to package directions, until soft, then drain and set aside.

Pound the shallots and chilis together in a mortar with a pestle until smooth. Add the shrimp paste and pound until combined.

Bring the coconut milk to a boil in a pan over medium heat. Add the chili paste, stir, and boil for about 2 minutes. Add the sugar, tamarind, salt, and a pinch of black pepper and stir until combined and beginning to boil. Add the shrimp and cook for 1–2 minutes, until the shrimp turn pink and are cooked. Add the noodles and stir for 3–4 minutes, until thoroughly combined and the noodles are soft and the liquid has been absorbed. Add a little water if the liquid evaporates before the noodles are soft enough to serve. Serve with raw or steamed vegetables.

Fried Noodles with Chicken and Gravy

Serves 4
Cook time: 30 minutes

— 2 teaspoons soy sauce
— ⅓ cup (45 g) tapioca flour
— 14 oz/400 g chicken breast, cut into
  ¼-inch/½ cm strips
— 11 oz/300 g Chinese egg noodles
— 4 tablespoons vegetable oil, plus
  extra for drizzling
— 4 cloves garlic, crushed
— 6 cups (1.5 liters) chicken stock
— 1½ tablespoons salted soybeans
— 1 tablespoon soy sauce
— ⅓ cup (75 ml) oyster sauce
— 1 tablespoon granulated sugar
— 1 teaspoon black pepper
— 9 oz/250 g bamboo shoots in brine,
  drained and cut into ½-inch/1 cm
  batons
— 1 can (5 oz/150 g) button mushrooms,
  drained

For garnish and serving
— 2 scallions (spring onions), cut into
  ½-inch/1 cm batons
— 4–5 fresh red chilis, seeded
— condiments, such as sugar, chili flakes,
  fish sauce, and white vinegar.

Combine the soy sauce and 1 tablespoon of the flour. Add the chicken and mix to coat. Cover the bowl and set aside for 10 minutes. Meanwhile, cook the noodles according to package directions in boiling water. Drain and transfer to a serving plate. Drizzle with oil and set aside.

Heat the 4 tablespoons oil in a wok over medium heat. Add the garlic and cook for 1 minute. Add the chicken, raise the heat slightly, and cook for 2–3 minutes. Add the stock and bring to a boil. Add the soybeans, soy sauce, oyster sauce, sugar, and pepper. Reduce the heat and simmer for 5 minutes.

Stir the remaining flour with ⅓ cup (75 ml) water until smooth. Raise the heat to medium and gradually add the flour mixture. Add the bamboo shoots and mushrooms, bring to a boil, and cook for 2–3 minutes.

Spoon the chicken and gravy over the noodles and garnish with the scallions and chilis. Serve with the condiments in separate bowls.

ผัดเส้นจันทร์

Fried Noodles

Serves 10
Cook time: 25 minutes, plus soaking time

For the chili paste
— 4 oz/100 g dried red chilis, seeded
— 10 shallots, chopped
— 2 bulbs garlic, cloves separated,
  peeled, and chopped
— 1 tablespoon salt

For the noodles
— 2 lb 4 oz/1 kg dried rice noodles
— 4 tablespoons vegetable oil
— 2 lb 4 oz/1 kg blue crabs, cleaned
— 1¼ cups (300 ml) Tamarind Puree
  (page 32)
— 1½ cups (300 g) jaggery, palm sugar,
  or light brown sugar
— 1 lb 2 oz/500 g raw shrimp (prawns),
  peeled and deveined

For serving
— 7 oz/200 g Chinese chives, snipped
  (about 5 cups)
— 1½ cucumbers, peeled and cut into
  lengthwise chunks
— 5 cups (1 lb 2 oz/500 g) bean sprouts

To make the chili paste, soak the dried chilis in a bowl of warm water for 15 minutes or until rehydrated, then drain and chop. Pound the chilis, shallots, garlic, and salt in a mortar with a pestle (or pulse in a food processor until smooth).

Meanwhile, to make the noodles, soak them in a bowl of water for 10 minutes, until soft. Drain, rinse, and set aside.

While the noodles are soaking, heat 1 tablespoon of the oil in a wok over high heat. Add the crabs and cook for 6 minutes. Remove from the pan and discard the oil. When cool enough to handle, cut into about 1½-inch/4 cm picces. Set aside.

In the same wok, heat the remaining 3 tablespoons oil over medium heat. Add the chili paste and stir-fry for 1 minute. Add the tamarind and sugar and simmer for about 3 minutes, stirring until the sugar has dissolved. Add the crab pieces and stir-fry for 2 minutes. Add the shrimp, noodles, and a few snipped chives, then reduce the heat to low and cook for 3–4 minutes. Serve with the remaining chives, the cucumbers, and bean sprouts.

ข้าวหอมมะลิ

Steamed Jasmine Rice

Serves 4
Cook time: 30 minutes

— 2 cups (14 oz/400 g) jasmine rice

Wash the rice and drain in a sieve. Transfer to a large pan, pour in 2½ cups (550 ml) water to cover, and bring to a boil over medium heat. Reduce the heat to low, cover, and cook for 20–25 minutes, stirring occasionally, until the rice is soft. Serve.

Desserts

Central Thailand is recognized as the birthplace of most
Thai desserts, many of which can be traced to the Portuguese
influence in the seventeenth century. Today sweets are sold at
stalls throughout Thailand, often laced with coconut, pandan,
or bananas. Even ice cream makes cameos in Thailand,
sometimes sold in "sandwiches" popped into hot dog buns,
topped with crushed peanuts, chocolate syrup, condensed
milk, and corn. The desserts in this section, though, hew
to more classic flavors and textures: pandan pudding, fried
bananas, tapioca, and melon dreamily lazing in coconut milk.

Tapioca with Longan

Serves 4
Cook time: 20 minutes

— 1 cup (7 oz/180 g) small tapioca pearls
— ½ cup (100 g) superfine (caster) sugar
— 1 cup (6 oz/170 g) longans in syrup,
  peeled and seeded, drained
— 1¼ cups (300 ml) coconut milk
— ¼ teaspoon salt

Bring about 5 cups (1 liter) water to a boil in a pan over medium-high heat.

Put the tapioca pearls in a sieve and dip in cold water, then shake once. Add to the pan of boiling water and cook for about 7 minutes, stirring occasionally, until the tapioca pearls are cooked and translucent. Remove from the heat and drain. Return to the pan, add the sugar and longans and gently stir over low heat until the sugar has dissolved.

Heat the coconut milk and salt in a separate pan over low heat for about 5 minutes. Transfer the tapioca and longan mixture to a serving bowl and pour the coconut milk over it. Serve.

Pandan Pudding

Serves 4
Cook time: 20 minutes

— vegetable oil, for greasing
— 10 pandan leaves
— ½ cup (80 g) rice flour
— 1 tablespoon mung bean flour
— 1½ tablespoons tapioca flour
— 1 cup (250 ml) club soda (soda water)
— 1½ tablespoons granulated sugar
— ⅓ cup (75 g) jaggery, palm sugar,
   or light brown sugar
— 1 cup (3 oz/80 g) grated fresh coconut,
   for serving

Grease a 8½ × 11-inch/21.5 × 28 cm rimmed baking sheet with oil and set aside.

Put the pandan leaves and 1 cup (250 ml) water in a food processor and blend until smooth. Drain the pandan juice through a fine-mesh sieve into a bowl and discard the solids.

Mix the flours together in a wok or pan, then gradually add the club soda, stirring constantly. Add the pandan juice and stir until smooth. Add the sugars and stir again until thoroughly combined. Put over medium heat and stir constantly until the mixture begins to thicken. Reduce the heat slightly and stir until shiny, solid, and dark green in color. This will take 7–8 minutes in total.

Pour the mixture onto the prepared baking sheet and use a spatula to spread the mixture over the surface. Let cool, then cut into 2½-inch/6 cm squares. Serve sprinkled with the grated coconut.

กล้วยทอด

Fried Bananas

Serves 6
Cook time: 30 minutes

— 1 tablespoon superfine (caster) sugar
— ¾ cup (120 g) rice flour
— ¼ cup (30 g) all-purpose (plain) flour
— ⅔ cup (2 oz/45 g) unsweetened shredded (desiccated) coconut
— 1 cup (250 ml) coconut milk
— 2 tablespoons white sesame seeds
— 1 teaspoon salt
— 6–8 semiripe small bananas, peeled and sliced into 1 ½-inch/4 cm lengths
— 5 cups (1 liter) vegetable oil, for deep-frying

Mix the sugar, flours, coconut, coconut milk, sesame seeds, salt, and ½ cup (120 ml) water together in a large bowl until the sugar and flour have dissolved.

Dip the bananas into the batter and make sure they are well coated.

Heat the oil in a wok or deep-fryer to 350°F/180°C or until a cube of bread browns in 30 seconds. Deep-fry the bananas for 6–7 minutes, until golden and crispy, then remove with a slotted spoon and drain on paper towels. Serve.

Muskmelon in Coconut Milk

Serves 6–8
Cook time: 15 minutes

— scant 1 cup (200 ml) coconut milk
— 1 cup (225 g) jaggery, palm sugar,
  or light brown sugar
— 1 teaspoon salt
— 1 muskmelon, cantaloupe, or
  honeydew melon, peeled, seeded,
  and cut into bite-size pieces
— crushed ice cubes, for serving

Heat the coconut milk in a pan over low heat.
Add the sugar and salt and stir constantly until
it comes to a gentle boil. Remove from the heat
and let cool.

Put about 7 melon cubes in a dessert bowl.
Add the coconut milk syrup and some crushed
ice cubes and serve.

Cooking Time Index

5 Minutes

10 Minutes

15 Minutes

20 minutes

25 minutes

30 minutes

Index

Phaidon Press Limited
Regent's Wharf
All Saints Street
London N1 9PA

Phaidon Press Inc.
65 Bleecker Street
New York, NY 10012

phaidon.com

First published 2017
© 2017 Phaidon Press Limited

ISBN 978 0 7148 7322 0

A CIP catalogue record for this book is available from
the British Library and the Library of Congress.

Commissioning Editor: Emilia Terragni
Project Editor: Laura Loesch-Quintin
Production Controllers: Nerissa Vales, Sue Medlicott
Design: Atlas
Cover Design: João Mota
Photography: Jean-Pierre Gabriel

Printed in Italy

The publisher would like to thank Yewande
Komolafe, Alexandra Van Buren, Kate Slate, Cecilia
Molinari, and Gemma Wilson for their contributions
to the book.

The author expresses his gratitude to the teams that
have supported him during his travels throughout
Thailand, as well as to the teams at the Office of
Agricultural Affairs, Royal Thai Embassy, Brussels.

RECIPE NOTES

Mushrooms should be wiped clean.

Eggs are assumed to be large.

Exercise a high level of caution when following
recipes involving any potentially hazardous activity,
including the use of high temperature and open
flames. In particular, when deep-frying, add the food
carefully to avoid splashing, wear long sleeves, and
never leave the pan unattended.